THE GOOGLE BOOK

V. C. VICKERS

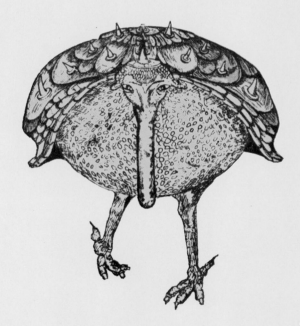

Oxford New York Toronto Melbourne

OXFORD UNIVERSITY PRESS

1979

FOREWORD

VINCENT Cartwright Vickers, my grandfather, and son of Alfred Vickers, founder of Vickers Armstrong, was born on 16 January 1879. His first wife died after only two years of marriage. They had a daughter, Wilma Countess of Cawdor. He and his second wife, whom he married in 1910, had two sons and four daughters. He was a devoted family man who was always at his most relaxed in the company of children. He went to Eton and then to Magdalen College, Oxford, and became an economist of considerable distinction and energy. He was a Deputy Lieutenant of the City of London, and a director both of Vickers Ltd and of the London Assurance. At the age of 31 he was appointed a director of the Bank of England, a post from which he resigned nine years later in protest at the then Governor's policy.

For the rest of his life he devoted himself to the cause of monetary reform, to the extent that a few days before his death after a long illness in 1939 he wrote, 'My keen desire to help up to the end has been the sole incentive which still enabled me to carry on perhaps a few weeks longer.' His book, *Economic Tribulation*, on which he was working right up to his death, was posthumously published in 1941 by John Lane, The Bodley Head.

He was a Fellow of the Royal Zoological Society and was interested in all animals, especially birds, which he studied in great detail. He even became a thoroughly proficient bird-call mimic. He was liable to paint birds wherever he was and on any material, once changing the snipe on his Humber Snipe car into one of his exotic inventions. Painting and drawing were relaxations to him. He had no formal training in art. The Google birds, most of which he painted when he was a young man, he first sketched roughly in pencil and then filled in with mapping pens and Indian inks. Some of them were exhibited in Gieves Art Gallery in Bond Street, London, in 1926 and at the Royal Academy in the same year. Unfortunately the originals of all those that were published are lost.

The Google Book itself was published in 1913 in a limited edition of one hundred copies when he was 34. A selection from that edition was further published in 1931 (at five shillings!). This new selection of the funniest verses and most appealing pictures seems to me to reflect admirably today's taste.

It is also a curious coincidence that Vincent Cartwright Vickers's grand-daughter is married to the present Earl of Clarendon, descendant of the famous 1st Earl after whom the Clarendon Press, the imprint of the Academic Division of Oxford University Press, was called.

Edward A. Dawson
Kirtlington, Oxon. 1979

THE GOOGLE BOOK

FAR! FAR away, the Google lives, in a land which only children can go to. It is a wonderful land full of funny flowers, and birds, and hills of pure white heather.

The Google has a beautiful garden which is guarded night and day. All through the day he sleeps in a pool of water in the centre of the garden; but when the night comes, he slowly crawls out of the pool and silently prowls around for food.

All the birds try to avoid the Google, because they don't like him and he frightens them; but some of them he can never catch, especially those with the red beaks. You can never see these birds anywhere except in Google land which is far far away, and only children can go there; and even they must be nearly – but not quite – asleep.

Now in this book you will find pictures of Google birds; some, though ugly, are very nice; others, though pretty, are very nasty. So, perhaps, really the pretty ones are ugly and the ugly ones pretty!

Who can tell?

THE GOOGLE'S GARDEN

Now on the facing page you see
The Google's garden (looking East);
The animal, that sits on guard,
Is quite a harmless little beast.
Please note the 'Pleecemen Birds' as well
On either side stand sentinel.

THE LESSER NOCKIT

How can one describe this remarkable bird
Which no one has seen and which everyone's heard;
It hammers and knocks on the trees and the rocks,
And batters and raps at the windy,
And rattles old bones and shuffles the stones
And kicks up a terrible shindy
               And hullaballoo!
It never stops still and it makes people ill
With its nerve-racking ear-splitting cry,
Which it utters they say both by night and by day,
And really I cannot think why!
               No more can you!

THE TANGO

The Tango trips upon her toes,
(That's why she's called the Tango)
And if you tease her, off she goes
As quickly as she can go!

THE BROWN WILLY

Just look at Brown Willy
Now isn't he silly?
He's just caught an eel in the water!
He'll throw it up high
Right into the sky
To be caught in the air by his daughter!

(Those two little things are *flies*,
not aeroplanes)

THE SUN BIRD

That great head, at any rate for me, has
    Positively no attraction,
And its general appearance gives one
    Very little satisfaction.
Yet what perspicacity we find there
    Hidden in his ugly brain-pan.
Keen wits a lunatic may have too,
    Just the same as any sane man.

(I can't understand a word of this,
    can you Mother ?)

THE LEMONSQUEEZER

Have you seen the Lemonsqueezer
Feeding Herbert and Louisa?

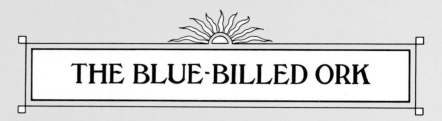

THE BLUE-BILLED ORK

This excessively conceited bird spends all his time looking for starfish, jellyfish, and crabs, and when he sees one near him he just loosens his neck and lets his beak drop.

You can't see any starfish or crabs in the picture because he isn't hungry just now.

O! little crab, O! little crab,
Be careful where you walk,
Or you may find yourself inside
The Tummy of the Ork!

THE FLABBYTOES

But mark!! What is that sound I hear?
Someone in agony I fear! –
Oh no!! It is old Flabbytoes,
You can't mistake his funny nose.

THE SHIVVER·DOODLE

To break the ice in wintry climes and dive into
    the Sea
To get one's food at feeding times, does not
    appeal to me.
If I liked fish, I would not wish to eat it raw
    and chew it,
But then you see I am not he, cos' he has *got* to
    do it.

GREAT SKULL-HEADED STONE TROT

With ponderous tread he walks for miles
And miles amongst the stones,
Searching along the sandy shore
For fossils shells and bones.

And when the wind is moaning
And the night is very dark,
If you listen at the window
You can sometimes hear him, – Hark!

THE POGGLE

The Poggle, as you have probably heard,
Is also known as the Pineapple Bird.
By nature he is soft and gently kind
To smaller birds who love his fruity mind.
So tame that he will feed out of your hands.
(He lives exclusively on wasps with yellow
    bands.)

THE GREAT McDOO OR DEWAR BIRD

The Great McDoo, aged ninety-nine,
Is rare but *very* cold,
And even in the winter time
Is thirsty so I'm told.

THE JUNKET

The little Junket spots his food
From almost any altitude,
Volplanés from an awful height
And plunges almost out of sight!

THE LITTLE HORN BACK

This funny thing lives in a part of Google Land where there are dreadful Landslips and Avalanches.

When he hears the roar of an approaching Avalanche, he snuggles in under his hard horny back and just waits for trouble. But the falling rocks and stones slide over his back and only make him tickle.

Sometimes he gets completely covered up and remains buried for several weeks, but he always crawls out all right, for no Little Horn Back has ever been hurt by a mere Avalanche!

THE SWANK

The Swank is quick and full of vice,
He tortures beetles also mice.
He bites their legs off and he beats them
Into a pulp, and then he eats them.

THE WILYOU OR PAGODA BIRD

Now if you said
When you're in bed,
'Ah Wilyou,
'Will you sing?'
He would reply
'Ononoti,'
And quickly take to wing.

THE SOFT-NOSED WOLLOP

The Soft-nosed Wollop lives on ice,
(In summer, Halibuts and Soles)
And when it's slippery he turns
Upon his back and rolls.

THE MIRABELLE

Old sailors have a tale they tell,
How once the song of a Mirabelle
Enticed a ship upon the rocks
Where perished all the crew.
I think it most improbable
That such a bird would cast a spell
Upon a ship, don't you ?

THE GOGO OR CAMEL BIRD

Now this is one of the largest birds to be found in all Google Land, and there really is not room enough for his body in the picture.

He eats most every living thing, and especially little young birds that can hardly fly.

He is horribly cruel, and no one (not even the Google itself) wants him to remain in Google Land.

That's why they call him Gogo.

THE GOOGLE'S GARDEN

(Looking West)

Which view d'you think the prettiest?

The sun is setting —
Can't you hear
A *something* in the distance
                    Howl!!?
I wonder if it's —
Yes!! it *is*
That horrid Google
On the prowl!!!

Oxford University Press, Walton Street, Oxford OX2 6DP

OXFORD LONDON GLASGOW
NEW YORK TORONTO MELBOURNE WELLINGTON
KUALA LUMPUR SINGAPORE JAKARTA HONG KONG TOKYO
DELHI BOMBAY CALCUTTA MADRAS KARACHI
NAIROBI DAR ES SALAAM CAPE TOWN

© The Estate of V. C. Vickers 1979

Designed by Sue Tipping

British Library Cataloguing in Publication Data
Vickers, V C
The google book.
I. Title
821'.9'12 PZ8.3 79 40165
ISBN 0 19 279735 2

*Printed in Great Britain by
Cox and Wyman Ltd., London, Fakenham, and Reading*

West Coast Modern

West Coast
Modern

Architecture, Interiors & Design

Zahid Sardar | Photographs by Matthew Millman

GIBBS SMITH
TO ENRICH AND INSPIRE HUMANKIND

First Edition
16 15 14 13 12   5 4 3 2 1

Text © 2012 Zahid Sardar
Photographs © 2012 Matthew Millman, except aerial image on
page 151 © Kevin G. Smith, photographer. Used by permission.

Library of Congress Cataloging-in-Publication Data
Sardar, Zahid, author.
  West Coast modern : architecture, interiors & design / Zahid
Sardar ; photographs by Matthew Millman. — First Edition.
     pages cm
  Includes bibliographical references.
  ISBN 978-1-4236-2439-4
1. Architecture, Domestic—Pacific Coast (U.S.)—
History—21st century. 2. Interior decoration—
Pacific Coast (U.S.)—History—21st century.
I. Millman, Matthew, illustrator. II. Title.
  NA7225.S27 2012
  728.0979—dc23
                          2012015348

Published by
Gibbs Smith
P.O. Box 667
Layton, Utah 84041

1.800.835.4993 orders
www.gibbs-smith.com

Designed by Zahid Sardar Design

Printed and bound in Hong Kong

Gibbs Smith books are printed on either recycled,
100% post-consumer waste, FSC-certified papers
or on paper produced from sustainable
PEFC-certified forest/controlled wood source.
Learn more at www.pefc.org.

PAGES 2–3: Matthew Trzebiatowski home and
blank studio office in Phoenix, Arizona.
PAGES 4–5: Idaho outpost for artist Jan Cox by
Seattle architect Tom Kundig.
FRONTISPIECE: Artist Ann Hamilton's double helix
tower installed by
Jensen Architects at the
Oliver Ranch in Geyserville, California.
THIS PAGE: Norah and Norman Stone's Calistoga,
California, art cave by Bade Stageberg Cox.

"*The West is still nascent, still forming, and that is where much of its excitement comes from. . . . It has a shine on it.*"

— Wallace Stegner

Contents

Introduction

A MODERN FRONTIER

ABOVE: In Los Angeles, California, skateboarders at a Venice Beach rink symbolize the area's free-spirited art community.
FACING: Nearby, architect Frank Gehry's 1984 Venice Beach house for Bill and Lynn Norton is another iconoclastic landmark.

The West is a place for adventurers and early adopters. It embraces the new. However, the vast stretch of North American West from Wyoming down to Arizona and out to the Pacific Coast, which the late author Wallace Stegner described as still forming, shining and new, is also infused with a Mesoamerican and Spanish Missionary spirit.

Those ancient strains meld neatly today with an effervescent modernity that is epitomized in the work of technology pioneers in the San Francisco Bay Area and the Pacific Northwest, by maverick performers and skateboarders alongside equally exhibitionist buildings on the boardwalk in Venice, California, where an artist community that included Ed Moses, Jean-Michel Basquiat and Ed Ruscha has long thrived, and by the boundless, futuristic imagination of Hollywood.

The homes included in this book represent the hybrids of old and new that periodically emerge along the coast, in deserts, up mountains and even across the ocean, where, for instance, Mexican-style courtyards morph into island lanais.

Early twentieth-century Southern California buildings by giants such as Irving Gill and architect Frank Lloyd Wright, whose influence spread from his Taliesin School in Scottsdale, Arizona, all the way to Hawaii and Japan, have had many descendants. Some of Wright's experiments with humble cinder block, such as his 1924 Ennis House in Los Angeles that consciously echoes the patterns and massing of Mayan temples and the sheltered courtyards of Mexican *ranchos,* are seminal. Austrian architects Rudolph Schindler and Richard Neutra, who adopted Los Angeles as home, admired, like Wright, California's breathtaking vistas and existing hybrid vocabulary and added to it their version of the clean-lined International style. They influenced others, such as Gregory Ain, whose modest, proletarian open-plan courtyard homes suited for clement weather became a part of the broad western

vernacular that would later fill expanding suburbs.

As the West commemorates the 75th anniversary of the Golden Gate Bridge—its symbolic gateway to modernity—it also recognizes the catalytic effect of the Japanese attack on Pearl Harbor just five years after the bridge was built. That act transformed the relatively isolated West Coast into an armed frontier with bunkers ready for war. New suburbs for soldiers on the coast rapidly replaced farmland and orchards, and by the end of World War II, California, Oregon and Washington, as well as their neighboring states, emerged as a thriving, modern international frontier between east and west with clusters of ranch-style homes.

Among them, Cliff May's typical ranch-style designs evolved from his San Diego family's Hispano-Moresque courtyard home and his own European, Spanish Colonial and Mexican roots. Built with only some discernible

Mediterranean and North African Moorish features to interrupt wood-framed stucco walls, large expanses of glass, low-slung roofs and broad verandahs, May's light-filled courtyard ranch houses shaped for modern open-plan indoor/outdoor living still resonate as new.

In 1945, when *Arts & Architecture* magazine editor John Entenza promoted the Case Study program to further improve the look of suburban buildings, more polished hybrids surfaced from the studios of architects Neutra, Schindler, Ray and Charles Eames, and many others, effectively influencing developers like Joseph Eichler in Northern and Southern California. Their prefabricated courtyard bungalows made wood, steel and concrete the new adobe.

Architects and developers incorporated clean-lined International style strictures "pragmatically and incrementally" to create regional arcadian suburbia, as Gwendolyn Wright,

FACING: An artist community embraces graffiti in Venice, California, where a beachside wall has been reserved for the art form. ABOVE: As if echoing her Southern California roots, San Francisco Bay Area art collector Chara Schreyer showcases art as arresting as graffiti, including floor art called *In Between False Comforts* by Robert Melee, an exploded Barbie dress in a cage by E. V. Day called *Bridal Supernova 1,* and, in the niche, Pierre-Louis Pierson's *La Comtesse de Castiglione (Cactus).*
RIGHT: Away from the glare of Hollywood, two semisuburban buildings remodeled by the Santa Monica firm Daly Genik face each other across a central courtyard that is entered through a side gate from the street. The atypical site plan reflects other Mediterranean and North African–style courtyard precedents along the Spanish Mission Trail. Filigreed, painted metal scrims like Arab *mashrabiyas* on all sides let in light yet provide privacy between the two buildings.

professor of architecture at Columbia University, succinctly describes in her foreword to *Eichler: Modernism Rebuilds the American Dream.*

Such eclectic environments became instructive backdrops for a new generation of architects and designers that helped to shape suburban Palm Springs and altered vibrant, vastly different cities such as Los Angeles and ever-denser San Francisco, cities in the greater Bay Area, in Silicon Valley and also, by extension, affluent technology constellations in Seattle, Washington, and coastal Vancouver, British Columbia, where modernist architect Arthur Erickson made his mark.

In the post-war years, when a shortage of housing for returning soldiers fueled more innovation, experimental ideas that allowed living outdoors as well as indoors—making small spaces seem bigger—spread north from the

Mexico/California coast, along the Spanish Mission Trail, all the way to Canada and Alaska, and out across the Pacific to Hawaii, where some mainlanders chose to remain.

Vladimir Ossipoff, a Russian American who had grown up in Japan and studied in California before he moved to Honolulu, came, it is said, to "wage a war on [presumably suburban] ugliness." He fashioned a tropical International style during the 1940s and 1950s. His sweeping, vaguely Japanese gabled roofs and whitewashed Mission-style architecture is also Wrightian with its intuitive mix of Arts and Crafts aesthetics and modern forms.

In the Bay Area, William Wurster picked up that refrain

FACING, TOP AND BOTTOM: Architect Vladimir Ossipoff's 1966 Davies Memorial Chapel in Hawaii combines a clean-lined aesthetic with raw and crafted details that are traditional.

RIGHT, TOP: The late Mexican architect Ricardo Legorreta also evoked Spanish Mission architecture in Hawaii.

RIGHT: Interstice Architects' spare, decorative steel, wood and acrylic stair in San Francisco echoes Arab oriel screens.

BELOW: In California Wine Country, Bay Area architect Peter Pfau's modern nod to Mediterranean courtyard pools.

ABOVE: Southern California architect Steven Ehrlich consciously embellishes North African–style courtyard compounds with modernist gestures akin to those of midcentury Case Study architects Richard Neutra and Rudolph Schindler. A white stucco box above the indoor/outdoor vestibule Ehrlich designed with Takashi Yanai, who brings a Japanese sensibility to the building, seemingly rests on striated glass fencing. FACING: San Francisco firm Pfau Long's similar illusion in the Wine Country incorporates its rocky, wooded site. A wood-clad cube opens onto a boulder that seems to support it.

of woodsy simplicity married to modern rigor during the 1940s and '50s and sculpted a regional Bay Area modernism. Landscape designer Lawrence Halprin's plan for Sea Ranch, a 1960s retreat along the Sonoma coast, 100 miles north of San Francisco, turned the West's gaze more emphatically to the outdoors. The environmentally attuned buildings that Halprin's colleagues William Turnbull, Charles Moore, Joseph Esherick, Donlyn Lyndon and Richard Whitaker designed there set the stage for a different kind of stew and a more green-minded western style that even the heavy-timbered Arts and Crafts–style modernism of the Northwest, Canada and Alaska would assimilate.

The organic, spontaneous thrusts of nature—and even graffiti, which could be considered "natural" art—inspired architects and interior designers in the West. Wright's buildings—fused to their sites—found new admirers.

During the 1980s, Canadian American architect Frank Gehry, who was drawn to white bungalows, chain-link fences, palm trees and eclectic buildings by Wright, Schindler and the Eameses in Los Angeles, added his own chapter of Deconstructivist, pop eclecticism that responds to site. His iconic 1984 Venice Beach house for art collectors Lynn and William Norton resembles a lifeguard station with a Japanese-style torii made of reused telephone poles.

Sculptural architects Thom Mayne and Eric Owen Moss, whose structures twist, turn and writhe "naturally" within their skins in nearby Culver City, were also influential. Daly Genik's filigreed metal mesh cloaks over two boxy buildings included herein surely owe them some credit.

In sum, the West, untethered to a single history, welcomes all ideas that work, and even the most modern and futuristic buildings in this book access a common western architectural genetic memory. Spare midcentury-style forms are sparked with handcrafted, woven details, green, energy-saving features and new technology. And, in the generation of Steve Jobs, Paul Allen, Facebook and Twitter, the West Coast modern frontier is wired for the future. □

BattersbyHowat's Gambier Island, British Columbia retreat.

Coast

Aptos House, California

EHRLICH ARCHITECTS

Courtyard houses lend themselves to communal, outdoor living, and Maybeck Award–winning Los Angeles architect Steven Ehrlich learned this early in his career as a Peace Corps volunteer in parts of West Africa. Ehrlich's own 2004 courtyard home in Los Angeles has proven instructive.

"Its simplicity is sheer beauty," said Leland Zeidler, an extroverted entrepreneur and real estate developer. One look at Ehrlich's house convinced Zeidler, as well as his wife, Marian, that it was the kind of building they wanted on their bluff overlooking the Pacific Ocean in Aptos, California.

LEFT: Cinder-block and glass walls surround the courtyard and pool between the main house and guest pavilion.
BELOW: The front door; RHEINZINK panels cover the stair tower.

"My home has sliding doors that disappear, and over-hangs for shade that block out the sun. It really resonated with them," Ehrlich recalled. "They understood the transformative power of modern houses that open to the outdoors."

Travelers, bon vivants and gourmets with a taste for wine, especially from Dordogne, France, where they have a second home, the Zeidlers asked Ehrlich to design an informal enclave to share with visitors, including their four grown children and three grandchildren.

The Zeidlers' generous, convivial lifestyle meshed well with Ehrlich's notions about living in shared compounds. His design, in collaboration with Takashi Yanai, a principal at Ehrlich Architects, consists of two buildings: a main house and a guest pavilion—one at each end of a courtyard containing an alfresco kitchen and a swimming pool.

The aesthetic lies within the Modernist canon of California architects Rudolph Schindler and Richard Neutra, yet its

FACING AND RIGHT: A white stucco vestibule, striated glass fencing and asymmetrical pavers are paired with concrete floors inside. TOP: The ocean is just yards away from the house.

TOP, ABOVE AND RIGHT: Instead of just white rooms in white boxes, "We use different materials in a sculptural way," Ehrlich said. In the open kitchen/dining/living space a fireplace is clad with earthy, burnished concrete block to complement the patina of RHEINZINK metal panels outside.

Bainbridge Bunker, Washington

EGGLESTON|FARKAS ARCHITECTS

Restaurants, theaters and exhibition spaces in decommissioned army bases in coastal cities around the United States are now commonplace, but a hilltop house by Seattle architects Eggleston|Farkas on Bainbridge Island in Washington may be the only contemporary home atop an abandoned military bunker.

Architect John Eggleston had looked at several sites with his clients Christine and Scott Needham, but realized that this one, replete with the remnants of a 1904 lookout station for Fort Ward's artillery batteries defending Puget

LEFT: Built atop a bunker and steel platform, the wood-frame home is clad with stained cedar siding installed vertically.
BELOW: A tilted steel brace holds up the sharply canted roof.

Sound, was ideal. From its perch on a one-and-a-half-acre site on the driest, highest south-facing point on the island, the graffiti-covered ruin commanded strategic views.

"The price of the property was greatly reduced on the assumption that removing the bunker would cost a fortune," Eggleston said. "But as soon as I saw it I knew we were keeping it."

He was confident that even though parts of the bunker's concrete roof had caved in, its thick reinforced concrete walls that were constructed to army specifications could last another century. A new concrete garage was added alongside the historic bunker, and together they formed an ideal foundation for the new structure.

"We simply bolted steel posts to the extremely thick old walls," Eggleston said. A steel frame that hovers above the foundation became the building pad for a conventionally framed rectangular tubular structure that contains two levels of living spaces, capped by a shed roof that cants up toward the view and extends out beyond the building envelope to form a cantilevered rain canopy.

On the main level, an open-plan dining and living area leads to a front deck facing the sound and is flanked on the sides by storage walls that are punctured only by narrow windows for visual privacy.

"Because there was limited buildable space on the heavily wooded site, we had to make the house extremely compact and focus it out to water views," Eggleston said. "The unobtrusive storage cabinets make the walls look really thick and the windows seem brighter."

"Drywall gets too damp up here. We try to avoid it," Eggleston said. So wall panels, floors, wall niches and even furniture the firm designed are all made of cherrywood.

Even cedar cladding under the canopy and the house, and vertical HardiePanel siding arranged in varying widths,

TOP: A galvanized steel and concrete front entry stair on the east side is weather resistant. LEFT: The historic concrete stairs. FACING: In this view, the house resembles a Japanese lantern.

BELOW AND RIGHT: Open-plan wood-clad living spaces take angular design cues from the original refurbished bunker below the house that is now a play space.

OVERLEAF: The kitchen forms a central core on the main floor. A hallway with built-in wall storage leads to a guest room. Blackened steel frames for the kitchen were made in situ and custom cherrywood cabinets were then slid into place.

ABOVE: The west side stairwell leads up to the bedrooms.
RIGHT: The secluded, quiet master suite. The deep roof over-hang helps to focus expansive views of Puget Sound.

are all either stained or painted to look like cherry or madrone bark. "We wanted the warmth of those colors to contrast with the gray weather," Eggleston said.

Inside, a central staircase leads up to bedrooms that can vary in height thanks to the extra headroom the metal shed roof provides. Because of that, Eggleston was also able to jog the floor of the master suite higher than the children's rooms on the other side of the central stairway. The gap between the stair landing and the master bedroom floor was big enough to add a band of windows from where the Needham children now happily peer into the living room.

The restored bunker has become a kind of fortress for the Needhams' two young children to play in. Only rac-coons, which are native to the rain-prone area, as are ferns, grasses, and fir, madrone and vine maple trees, can breach the bastion every once in a while. □

Belvedere Island House, California

PAUL WISEMAN

Despite its classical Mediterranean flavor, interior designer Paul Wiseman's elegantly simple, all-white weekend cottage brimming with cherished objects is what machine-for-living advocate Le Corbusier might have also called a "treasure chest of living."

Wiseman—a decorator for Fortune 500 CEOs and other luminaries such as conductor Michael Tilson Thomas—recently remodeled the 1912 cottage perched on a hill in Belvedere, a short drive north from San Francisco, although he has shared it with his partner, attorney Richard Neil Snyder, for more than a decade.

Their stucco-covered 1,600-square-foot cottage, which echoes villas along Lakes Como and Garda in Italy, was built as a weekend retreat for the well-traveled surgeon Florence Nightingale Ward, whose clinic was in San Francisco.

The five-room house, hidden along a walkway inaccessible to cars, has a bucolic setting amid its tiered succulent garden by Todd Cole interspersed with pergolas and decks. From its Tuscan-style loggia off the living room and the master suite on the main floor, there are views of Corinthian and Angel islands, Tiburon, Mount Tamalpais and Sausalito, as well as the Golden Gate Bridge, which spelled the end for regular ferry service from San Francisco to the islands a quarter century after the house was built.

"We needed to add a little more space and modern amenities, but instead of starting over, we wanted to save this building as a document of Bay Area architectural history," Wiseman said.

FACING: Wiseman's two-year-long renovation resulted in saving the cottage and loggia attributed to architect Julia Morgan. Modern latticed shutters allow bay views.
LEFT: Munder-Skiles teak furniture sits outside the living room.

Seemingly untouched, the once-rotting cottage, rumored to have been designed by turn-of-the-century architect Julia Morgan (the first woman admitted as a student of architecture at the École des Beaux-Arts in Paris), now has modern state-of-the art heating and wiring and, in lieu of a small storage pocket under the house, a proper foundation and a guest suite excavated from the hillside by hand, all ready for another century of use.

"Despite the inadequate construction, the cottage was perfectly designed. We simply added to its best features," Wiseman said. For instance, his firm, The Wiseman Group, which oversaw the architectural and engineering details of the project, added radiant heating under new wood floors, new bronze doors and windows with louvered wood shutters

LEFT: An octagonal table designed by Edwin Lutyens and reproduced by his heirs has wedge-shaped chairs around it.
BELOW: The eclectic living room is a showcase for seventeenth-century Jacobean chairs, new bronze doors and Reed sconces designed by The Wiseman Group and made by Phoenix Day.

and ample insulation, but they didn't change the original floor plan upstairs or the Rumford fireplace, "because it can heat the whole house when we want," Wiseman said.

Although the rooms have low ceilings, they made no attempts to change that greatly because, "The views are so big, the low ceilings create an intimacy you wouldn't expect," he said. Another aspect of the house that they left unchanged was its various loggias and garden terraces arranged to avoid the strong afternoon west winds. "You can move from loggia to loggia and benefit from the sun all day long," Wiseman said.

Adding only a small amount of space in a landlocked setting was expensive, but for Wiseman and Snyder adding a lot of space was never the goal.

"The size is right. The house is efficient and we use every part of it. I have gone into houses that are too big," said Wiseman. "This is a sustainable size and I bring clients here for a Sunday lunch so they can understand that."

Inside, Wiseman's trademark marriage of old and new aesthetics, so often pictured in the pages of glossy magazines like *Architectural Digest,* hints at Le Corbusier's own fascination with the Parthenon's proportions that led to the architect's distinctive modern spatial vision.

Wiseman's alchemy combines vintage objects from different periods, such as Jacobean furniture and designs by British Arts and Crafts architect Edwin Lutyens, with a portrait of Igor Stravinsky by Charley Brown and other contemporary art from his collection.

"If I have to give a name to my palette, it would be 'Appropriate,'" Wiseman said. "This is a summer house to relax in. To get to the house you have to walk through and up a garden path and leave the rest behind," he said. It has everything Wiseman and Snyder need, such as their collection of treasured English antiques including essentials like easy-to-care-for teak deck furniture, lounging sofas, daybeds, good lamps and things to read. "It is hard to leave such a place," Wiseman added. □

FACING: In the hillside garden, sheltered nooks offer refuge from the wind. The concrete fire pit reprises one by director Luis Ortega in Hollywood. TOP: The loggia, with its checkered pergola, is another spot to view the bay and Angel Island. ABOVE: Shades of white and yellow in the bedroom.

Gambier Island House, British Columbia

BATTERSBYHOWAT ARCHITECTS

The Gulf Islands scattered off the coast of British Columbia, a short boat ride away from west Vancouver, are a respite from city life by any measure, but a cabin on secluded Gambier Island designed by the young award-winning Vancouver firm BattersbyHowat offers something that exceeds that. It is—to paraphrase the late Canadian architect Arthur Erickson—modern architecture to assuage nature.

Indeed, it could be argued that it was nature that directed architects David Battersby and Heather Howat's design of this weekend hideout for a pair of television and film producers and their two young sons.

The owners' principal requirements—to create a sustainable version of their polished life in the city—were

TOP: The cabin is a hooded lens to view Howe Sound.
RIGHT AND FACING: Raised on concrete plinths, the house does tree roots little harm. Its slit windows have views of woods also echoed in vertical cedar cladding.

interpreted by the architects in a site-specific way. When they encountered an intransigent rock outcropping in the middle of the narrow, 80-foot-wide site, they left it undisturbed and decided to wrap the roughly 2,000-square-foot structure around it in the shape of a question mark. "In this way the house is not a monolith. It is set up as a point and counterpoint," Battersby said.

Responding to the sloped site that ends abruptly in a cliff face, the building steps down in three tiers toward the water. Pins cemented directly into the bedrock up high obviate the need for the kind of clunky footings a conventional foundation requires, and allow the long, telescopic open-plan living space in the front of the house to be cantilevered on a narrow plinth lower on the site. As a result, the house avoids harming tree roots and hovers over native foliage. Its front deck, shaded by the sloped roof that extends over it, is a spot to enjoy Howe Sound and the occasional dolphin. The master bedroom in back looks across the natural

ABOVE: The entry porch doubles as a sheltered mudroom with a built-in bench. RIGHT: The living room, with a RAIS stove, and the canopied front deck are aimed at views.

rock atrium formed by the crook of the house and, through the living spaces, at glancing views of the water beyond. Slit windows here and there capture views of the surrounding conifers and madrones.

The exterior, more rustic than a typical BattersbyHowat project, has random-width, rough-sawn, beveled, stained cedar siding installed vertically to mimic tree trunks. "The blackened siding will weather so it looks charred like bark," Battersby said. For contrast, and to extend the arboreal metaphor, "we used comparatively brilliant fir on the floors inside and unfinished hemlock on the ceilings where it is most protected," he said.

Nature had a hand in the construction as well. When the builders had to bring in plywood, lumber and other

BELOW: The tiered house wraps around a rock outcropping, providing a logical division of public and private space while allowing light into rooms in both sections.
RIGHT: The master suite looks across the divide, through the dining and living spaces, at views of the water.

materials—down to the last nail—they found they could only barge it in at high tide to a communal landing on another side of the island. Large structural steel components had to be flown in by helicopter because the grassy path from the landing to the site was too soft to handle the weight.

Now, a ramp that can be lowered by hand via weight-laden pulleys allows private boats or water taxis to dock directly below the house. From that perspective on the water, the clean-lined, darkened structure so keenly attuned to its site seems "like a long shadow in the woods," Battersby said.

Battersby has a great interest in landscape design, and together he and Howat have developed a reputation for just such site-specific solutions that lie between Erickson's poetic concrete abstractions and the Arts and Crafts–style

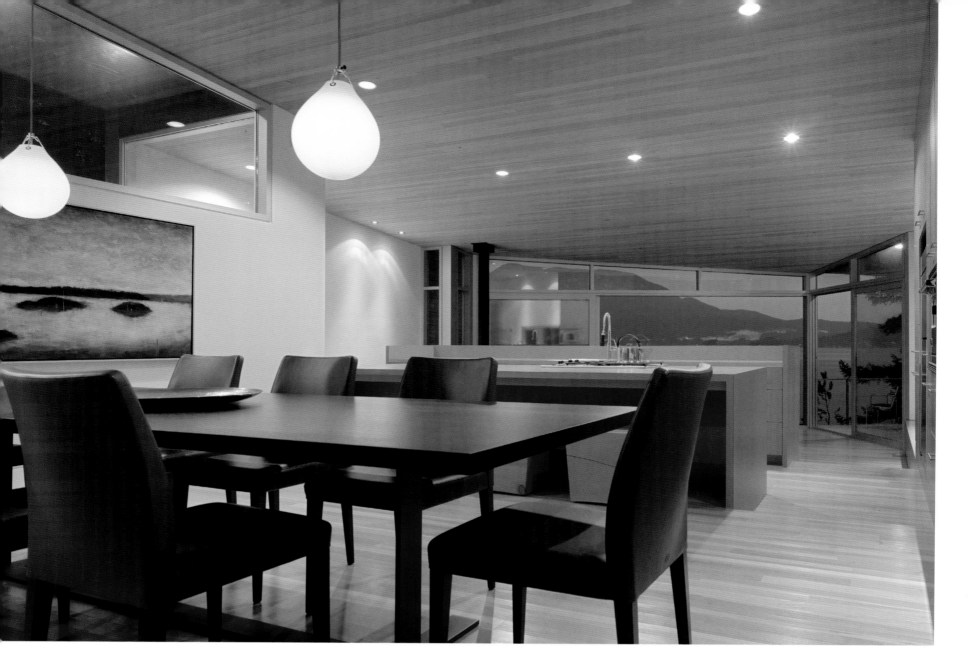

ABOVE: The dining areas step down to the living section.
FACING: In the master bath, mosaic-glass-tiled walls and floors
and a custom double vanity are practical features.

nature-conscious modernism of contemporary Canadian firms such as Helliwell + Smith: Blue Sky Architecture.

"We even replanted indigenous species after I consulted a horticulturist who worked for the government," Battersby said. He reseeded undergrowth, grasses and hedges using a customized seed mixture "that includes wildflowers that grow on other parts of the island."

The owners were drawn to these architects for a reason. According to Battersby, they are also keen environmentalists. The husband deployed his film set knowledge of mechanics and lighting to angle solar panels on the roof for optimum benefit. Septic tanks, generators and other off-grid systems, including collecting rain and stream water in tanks under the decks, were his domain. He also configured an insulating system of alternating foam baffles to minimize noise and reverberation from the power generators hidden in a bunker clad with similar materials as the house.

These were all important measures on the island, where roads are of dirt and there are no general stores, phones or essential services. In its way, the house is both instructive and demanding. Cooking, a hobby in the city, becomes a necessity when the owners want to eat fresh meals. For the children, jigsaw puzzles become the principal entertainment, and conservation is not just about gathering solar power and being off the grid, but determining just how much energy and electricity is essential for living well. □

Kona House, Hawaii

LEGORRETA + LEGORRETA / THE WISEMAN GROUP

The northwest Kona Coast of Hawaii is flooded with look-alike vacation homes and resorts surrounded by palm trees and lawns, but one earthy yellow house that belongs to an athletic couple from San Francisco carefully frames the ocean, stretches of black lava rock flecked with white coral and sculptural kiawe trees like a work of art.

The U-shaped structure surrounding a central courtyard is by the late Mexican architect Ricardo Legorreta, the winner of an American Institute of Architects Gold Medal award and Japan's 2011 Praemium Imperiale prize. It adheres to the same structural and setback guidelines as its neighbors along the bluff, however it derives its contemporary cubistic look from Mediterranean-style courtyard homes in Mexico, where Legorreta, like his mentor, Luis Barragán, was famous for abstracting Colonial Hispanic and pre-Columbian forms.

TOP: The tower portal leads to an entry courtyard with a pool.
RIGHT: In back, central living spaces, the master suite and guest rooms atop it face a beach of lava rock and white coral.

Courtyards and terraces, not visible from the street, break up the two-story, 12,000-square-foot home into public and private sections. Conceived as a walled compound, it comprises generously scaled convivial spaces to entertain a few friends or many. The two secluded second-story guest suites are up separate flights of stairs on the north and south sides of the central courtyard.

According to Legorreta, who designed all his projects with his son Victor, a partner in the firm Legorreta + Legorreta, courtyards allow for cross-ventilation and bring in light. "In such warm climates, courtyards become the

FACING: Wiseman's small dining tables can be joined.
ABOVE AND TOP: In the entry courtyard, a canted guest pavilion is visible beyond the dividing wall. Stepped seats of dark, lava-like granite and soft cushions frame a fountain pool.
RIGHT: Sunlit hallways between the wings double as galleries.

LEFT: The canted guest room is an island unto itself. The sound of falling water, and reflections ricocheting around the pool, are like a *son et lumiere* show. The pool flows around the left corner and abuts the guest bathroom shower door.

ABOVE: Glass doors slide open so guests can step into the foot-deep water that flows in from the entry courtyard pool. The entry tower is visible above the wall fountain.

center of a house and the main gathering space," Legorreta said just weeks before his death.

So the entry courtyard, entered through a dramatic tower portal with a handcrafted Cor-Ten steel door, has an inverted pyramidal fountain of black honed granite, and is also a place to sit and sip drinks. The courtyard leads directly into an art foyer that flows into an open-plan living and dining room that links to a porticated loggia with ocean views. On the north side of the rear patio, a plunge pool seems to tame the ocean, barely one hundred yards away, and bring it closer. That's important because, the architect explained, after dark the Pacific becomes "almost frightening."

A convex, sail-shaped roof of concrete above the lofty living space, which allows for shaded clerestory windows to bring in light, and a canopied lap pool within the master wing on the south side are distinctive touches that respond to the owners' love of sailing and swimming.

Freestanding walls to create outdoor spaces—a Legorreta hallmark—and more water features, such as wall fountains, liven other parts of the south wing, which is just wide enough for the master suite and a library with private decks facing west with views of the startling black beach and ocean. Within that wing, an east-facing guest room might have seemed less desirable had the architect not floated the canted, square-shaped room in a meditative pool of water surrounded by high walls that are animated by reflections that ricochet off the pool's rippling surface.

"We simply created for it its own relationship with water and now everyone wants to stay in this room," Legorreta said. Fighting the impulse to face every space toward the grandest view always has rewards, he added, because "a courtyard, a tree or a fountain can be as beautiful as the sea."

FACING: The canted bedroom's bathroom has mirrors laminated to glass walls. Its hewn stone vanities are freestanding. The shower back door opens to the wading pool. RIGHT, TOP: The owners' private pool. RIGHT: Stairs go up to a guest suite.

collected with the help of San Francisco interior designer Paul Wiseman, who has collaborated with the owners on previous homes in Sausalito and San Francisco.

"I create intimate space through scale," said Wiseman, who designed particular pieces of teak furniture, such as high-back slatted chairs inspired by the architecture, to form islands of privacy within open spaces.

All the custom pieces were made in Jakarta, Indonesia, where Wiseman and the owners also found many of the antiques, textiles and artifacts now displayed within the space.

"Most of the time it functions as a quiet retreat for my husband and myself," said one of the owners, happy that they resisted the temptation to build a house closer to Legorreta in Mexico. "We had been going to Mauna Kea Resort for many years and we loved this location," she said. "It is a place where we could set up our own way of life." □

The asymmetrical volumes of the poured-concrete house resemble those of white-walled villas on a Greek island. However, "We could not think of a more aggressive color in Kona than white; that is why we chose a more earthy yellow," the architect said.

Typically Legorreta liked to choose colors for the interiors last, walking through the finished all-white spaces of the houses he designed with Victor until he "felt" the right shade to accent a room. The architect's signature blood reds, fuchsia pinks, blues and purples—greatly toned down to complement the earthy muted shades of the house, concrete floors and Brazilian cherrywood cabinetry—define and highlight the mostly golden terra-cotta and soft white interiors of the open-plan living spaces and discrete bedrooms.

"The powder room is deep blue and pink and certain walls are painted a strong color, but I tend to like more neutral colors for a calm setting," said one of the owners, who worked closely with the architect on the scheme.

From a distance the house settles into its landscape. From inside it is a window to enjoy the views outside, and also a vitrine for Pacific island art and Chinese antiques

TOP: The convex concrete roof floats above living areas.
ABOVE: Wiseman's high-back benches, near the oceanside plunge pool, echo Legorreta's architecture.
RIGHT: In a guest room above the master suite, Richard Misrach's photograph of waves complements real ocean views.

Lagoon House, California

GARY HUTTON DESIGN

One of the few custom homes that 1950s architect A. Quincy Jones designed for California developer Joseph Eichler overlooks the beautiful lagoon dividing Belvedere Island from the Marin mainland near San Francisco. The modest home has been given a fresh start.

"I was looking for just such a house on the water," said influential art patron and collector Chara Schreyer, who chanced upon it in her search for a place to house art from the 1960s, when the home was built.

LEFT: Clerestory windows bring in light. A portrait of artist Joseph Beuys by Andy Warhol hangs on the chimney. Openings on each side lead to bedroom wings.

TOP: Schreyer's otherwise little-changed historic Eichler home on Belvedere Lagoon has a glossy new red front door.

While other Eichlers, as the developer's buildings came to be called, have not fared well, Schreyer's better-built 2,100-square-foot, single-story Belvedere home remained mostly intact, and is a prime example of western living from that era. It shares the characteristics of its less-expensive mass-produced brethren: an open floor plan, flat and peaked roofs, clerestory windows and large plate-glass walls.

Eichlers built in the 1960s were, technologically speaking, state of the art and well planned, with an atrium or interior courtyard for living indoors and out in the warm

ABOVE: Under the peaked section of the roof, the entryway and an atrium share fritted glass panel walls.
RIGHT: In the living room, a George Nelson Marshmallow sofa studs views of the lagoon. Vintage Pop cubist side tables and Artichoke pendant lamps by Poul Henningsen join a classic Raymond Loewy Picnic Blanket rug reissued by Edward Fields.

California milieu in which the two firms Eichler favored, Emmons and Jones, and Anshen + Allen, thrived. Their affordable, elegant solutions were especially timely during the postwar building boom, in which, coincidentally, Schreyer's father, a developer in Los Angeles and a friend of Eichler's, also had a hand.

With the help of architect Craig Hudson and interior designer Gary Hutton, who were guided by Jones's 1963 drawings of the house, Schreyer made a few obvious, necessary improvements to undo a previous owner's heavy-handed interventions such as Sheetrock over a signature

stone fireplace, and many invisible ones such as the new heating ducts and electrical systems that Hudson concealed in the imperceptibly thickened roof. A den that had been opened to the living room by the former owners was also restored to its former shape. Other changes include fresh kitchen surfaces and double-paned fenestrations instead of standard single-pane plate-glass windows that offered poor insulation.

The Corian countertops and Bisazza tile that the architect and interior designer used for the kitchen and bathrooms simply didn't exist in the 1960s. "But we were doing exactly what Eichler might have done. He loved to promote

FACING: A masonry chimney anchors the living spaces. Next to the kitchen in back, celadon green Saarinen chairs fill the dining alcove. Framed works include prints by George Platt Lynes. Round Warren Platner glass-and-wire side tables flank sofas by Florence Knoll.

ABOVE: The bedroom, with Flos Glo-Ball lamps by Jasper Morrison, showcases an image by Eija-Liisa Ahtila directly above the bed, and opposite it is one by Richard Prince.

LEFT: A Keith Tyson canvas hangs in the hallway. Original ceilings were untouched, but the roof was thickened to accommodate wiring and heating.

the latest materials and technology," Schreyer said, referring to Eichler's love of synthetic laminates and in-floor radiant heating in concrete floors.

Together these changes have made the home comfortable for both the collector and the art.

In its newest chapter as a museum, the structure joins Schreyer's unique collection and gives 1960s and 1970s works by pop artist Andy Warhol and conceptual works by Joseph Beuys, Man Ray, Marcel Duchamp, Diane Arbus, Donald Judd and Ed Ruscha an entirely new context.

Schreyer has also collected interior objects that give her new museum elements that subtly amplify the important, history-making era when Emmons and Jones conceived their timeless buildings. Hutton found rugs designed in 1946 by Raymond Loewy (famous for creating the iconic Coca-Cola and Pan Am logo designs) and reissued by luxury carpet maker Edward Fields. Also included are couches by Florence Knoll, who altered the way interior designers conduct business; a 1950s Marshmallow sofa by George Nelson, who responded to pop art's fascination with cans and bottle tops and helped open the way for conceptual furniture; and a coffee table by Hans Wegner, whose modern blend of Eastern and Western aesthetics is being reprised today in collaborations with Korean artists by Gijs Bakker, cofounder of Dutch design collective Droog.

As a finishing touch, contemporary furniture designed by Hutton and Bay Area designers Daven Joy and Chris Deam offer the artful belvedere an introspective vista of its past, present and future. □

FACING: In the den, an armchair by Carlo Mollino contrasts with Montis chairs around a vintage Ray and Charles Eames card table. *Potomac Parkway,* a vibrant gridded painting on the wall by Sarah Morris, alludes to the architecture of power. RIGHT, TOP TO BOTTOM: The master bedroom opens to the atrium; in the den, an Elizabeth Neel canvas; the kitchen has lagoon access and new Corian counters Eichler would like.

Venice Condo, California

GARY HUTTON DESIGN

"The location was absolutely perfect. It was close to Santa Monica, at the lower end of lively Abbot Kinney and near some of Frank Gehry's earliest buildings," Reno art dealer Peter Stremmel said, referring to the area in Venice, California, where he had invested in a townhouse condominium before it was built. When it finally neared completion, Stremmel and his wife, Turkey, decided to keep the pied-à-terre for themselves.

ABOVE: Above the entry door, Hutton designed a cut-steel canopy inspired by the Venice city grid. A powder room cloaked in black steel panels has graffiti painted inside.
RIGHT: Stairs connect the loft's two stories and mezzanine.

"When there is deep snow in Reno it is nice to come here, put on a pair of shorts and go to the beach," Stremmel said. "It is also a very funny place. The Venice Boardwalk is like Burning Man on training wheels."

There were other lures. The beach three blocks away might attract odd muscled men, head shops and skateboarders, but it has also nurtured some of California's greatest artists. For instance, Richard Diebenkorn's Ocean Park series was inspired by the view from his Venice studio. And artists Peter Alexander, Ed Ruscha, Larry Bell and Charles Arnoldi, who is one of the artists represented by Stremmel's gallery, live and work in the neighborhood.

ABOVE: Charles Arnoldi's lively mixed media artwork hangs above a sleek white sofa by Gary Hutton Design.
RIGHT: High-backed Sturgis chairs and an A6 coffee table are all from the Gary Hutton Furniture Collection. The seven-legged white Cloud Series side table is by Therien's Studio Workshops.

"In fact, Chuck Arnoldi is one of my best friends, and we were visiting him when we first saw the hole in the ground for our nine-unit building's foundation next door to him," Stremmel said.

They liked the idea of being his neighbor—far from gated communities in Beverly Hills or Bel Air—but when they finally got possession of their townhouse, they were quite disappointed. "It wasn't the high-end project we envisioned," Stremmel declared.

Enter award-winning San Francisco interior designer Gary Hutton, whose expertise is creating refined, understated

interiors to showcase art. "He had worked for us before and we knew he could spark up these rooms," Stremmel said.

Hutton altered a few walls, and with gallons of white paint transformed the 2,300-square-foot, two-and-a-half-story townhouse into one of the most interesting homes in the condominium compound.

"We tried to create a place that represented a real change from their colorful Mark Mack–designed home in Reno," Hutton said. "The Stremmels come to spend time at the beach and so the colors we used are bleached and subtle even in the furnishings."

"Although it is on Main Street facing the water, the townhouse has no view in particular. Where you have large windows, there are other buildings relatively close," Hutton said. "It's an inward-looking space. I knew white walls would work best."

For visual punch, he contrasted the yards and yards of white with neutral black accents. "We knew Peter's art would always change and so we needed inconspicuous backdrops. It was not as if I was Billy Baldwin designing a room around a single Goya painting," Hutton chuckled.

The design had to make room for Arnoldi, too.

"Arnoldi did constructions with twigs very early in his career, such as the one Michael Taylor used for Gorham and Diana Knowles's home in Lake Tahoe," Hutton said. He placed one of Arnoldi's 1980s originals in the living room, alluding to Taylor's version of California beach chic.

"It was a generic loft project that could have been anywhere, but we aimed to give it a local flavor and echoed the culture of that place," Hutton said. "I wanted something like the boardwalk to assault the senses at the entryway so I added a canopy that you have to walk under before you enter the tall two-and-a-half-story space. At first we considered layers of metal to create shadows, but then this gridded design emerged after I looked at a street map of the neighborhood."

Hutton also brought a bit of the street into the powder room off the foyer. He hired a local graffiti artist to decorate its all-black walls with free-form art.

In the mezzanine office, bookcase supports that look like barbells commonly seen on Muscle Beach have "Peter and Turkey's initials at the ends," Hutton said with a laugh.

FACING: Ray and Charles Eames dining chairs and a Saarinen table by Knoll mesh with a horse sculpture by Deborah Butterfield, artwork by Gregory Crewdson and a custom chandelier by Hutton. RIGHT, TOP: A desk chair by Mario Botta sits next to shelves with barbell-shaped supports by Hutton. RIGHT: A Fjord chair by Moroso; art by Peter Alexander.

Equally witty, in the living spaces on the main floor, "The crazy white, powder-coated steel and leather Sturgis chair I designed responds to Southern California's motorcycle culture," Hutton said. "It's my version of lowrider furniture." It is paired with classics such as Ray and Charles Eames chairs around the dining table as homage to their iconic home and office a few miles away in Pacific Palisades.

Hutton's humor and wit are coupled with practicality. "There is always sand and beach stuff to contend with," he said. "That was the main reason why we wanted it to be a low-care interior as well." So bare, smooth-troweled gray concrete floors were not dressed up, and the only rug Hutton added in the interior is made of gray sisal for "a California beachy feeling."

Even though the contractor-built loft building is nothing special, the interior is, and Stremmel, with his unerring collector's instinct, knows "there will never be a multifamily project built on such a parcel of land here again." □

LEFT: A voluptuous sofa, chairs and coffee table by Minotti, a vintage Swedish lamp, a rug from The Rug Company and a faceted side table by Hutton join Tony de los Reyes' diptych.
TOP: From the top floor, stairs continue up to the roof.

Waimea House, Hawaii

WALKER WARNER ARCHITECTS

The long, shed-roofed home that Greg Warner designed for a resort developer and his family in Hawaii draws as much inspiration from its upland cattle ranch setting beside a rain forest preserve near Waimea as it does from the nature-inspired modernism of the late Russian-American architect Vladimir Ossipoff, who lived and worked in Honolulu.

"My client had always been impressed by Ossipoff's sensibility, and when he learned that I had studied at Ossipoff's mid-century Hawaii Preparatory Academy we immediately clicked," Warner, a founder of the San Francisco firm

LEFT: A rear view of architect Greg Warner's Ossipoff-inspired ranch house near the Kona coast. Its sloped roofs and vertical wood siding reflect vernacular farm sheds.
ABOVE: It sits on an ecotone between dry and very rainy zones, so the path to the front door is also sheltered.

Walker Warner, said. "I consider Ossipoff's Davies Memorial Chapel on that campus the foundation of my own architectural direction."

With a corrugated tin roof, board-formed walls made of cement and lava rock, and indigenous Hawaiian wood posts, Ossipoff's 1966 chapel is powerfully simple and timeless.

"That's what more Hawaii architecture could be like," Warner said, lamenting the fact that the island's tropical, mid-Pacific climate more readily attracts overblown Balinese lanais and enormous California-style ranch houses.

ABOVE: A misty tableau of Mauna Kea, seen from the den on the drier side of the property, is ever changing.
RIGHT: A palette of hardwoods includes ipe for lanai decks and a solid ohia tree trunk post. Wood and glass doors slide back for alfresco living. Arts and Crafts–style kitchen cabinets visible inside echo Japanese tansus.

The developer and his wife did not want to dominate the hill or the view with a large, showy house, so their one-room-deep home made of wood and glass sitting on 20 acres is just 2,800 square feet and a single story high. It sits neatly on a ridge between two distinct microclimates, with native ohia myrtle trees and streams on one side and expansive, treeless stretches on the relatively dry side facing snow-capped Mauna Kea.

"It is also positioned for the weather," Warner said. Built on an east-west axis, the narrow building is impervious to strong winds that frequently blow in that direction.

TOP: Wood-framed glass windows and stone foundations liven the rear section of the house facing former grazing land.
RIGHT: When the central living room doors are slid back, the rear decks become a part of the living room. Doors to the partially visible forested front garden allow cross-ventilation.

ABOVE: Master bedroom windows facing east catch the first light and have unobstructed valley and mountain views.
FACING: A custom concrete tub in the master bathroom is fashioned like Japanese ofuro soaking tubs made of wood.

More such practicality abounds. Doors and windows are positioned to maximize cross-ventilation and eliminate the need for air conditioning or heating. A flat, standing seam steel shed roof, which slopes toward the natural watershed and streams in front of the house, is like others in the area.

"A pitched roof would have stood out too much. Sloped corrugated roofs are common for the amount of precipitation we get here," the developer said, adding, "we've even got a cedar ceiling to muffle the sound of rain."

Most of the time, the balmy weather encourages outdoor living. A large living and dining area with wall-size barn doors opens to a lanai sheltered by projecting bays on each side in the rear. This central space is flanked by a master suite on the east side and, at the opposite end, rooms for the owners' two children, who enjoy being close by.

"We wanted one big area in the middle to dine together every night," the developer said. "I grew up in a house in Southern California with a formal dining room but we never used it very much."

To further mesh the house with its landscape, most of its materials were selected to acquire a gradual patina. Inside, the red cedar will turn gray, and a naturally fluted, bark-covered ohia wood post outside—a clear nod to Ossipoff—will take on a charred, weathered sheen over time.

"It is well camouflaged in this context," Warner said.

From the carport, a covered walkway that goes past lush landscaping to a simple façade and a narrow front door adds another veil before you enter the house.

"It is a trick to reveal the view gradually," the developer said. Inside, three tall bay windows in back open to dramatic vistas of pastureland and the distant volcano.

"When you step inside you can see that the roof cants up, and you get a full view of the valley," the owner said. "When there is a tropical rainstorm and the sun comes out at the same time, it all looks simply extraordinary." □

At Chara Schreyer's San Francisco condo, Tony Feher's artful bottle sculpture *Because I Love It So Very Much*.

City

Venice Compound, California

DALY GENIK ARCHITECTS

The spirit of recycling and reuse of natural resources prevalent on the West Coast is alive in Venice, California, where Sam Laybourne, a young television and film comedy writer for Columbia and Fox and Herran Bekele, a former television news producer for ABC News, *Good Morning America* and *Nightline,* looked for a modest compound they could eventually refurbish. They found a Santa Fe–style stucco confection with a separate guesthouse they planned to share with Laybourne's parents, who are both retired entertainment media executives in New York City.

As Laybourne and Bekele's plans for a family grew, so did the plan to remodel. They knew that their main house, set at the rear end of its city lot and separated by a central courtyard from their street-side garage, and the older Laybournes' poorly planned 550-square-foot pied-à-terre, needed to change. The house in particular had an open loft bedroom that offered no privacy and only one other spare room squeezed into a former garage that used to open onto a back alley.

"At first it seemed like a pretty straightforward remodeling project," said architect Kevin Daly of the firm Daly Genik, which was hired to do the job.

Daly, a former student of architect Richard Fernau, of Fernau & Hartman Architects in Berkeley, who had designed two homes for Laybourne's parents, embarked on basic remodeling, but soon saw greater potential than that. "Both buildings were oriented toward the lushly planted courtyard between them, and that was an advantage," he said.

TOP, LEFT AND FACING: The family compound comprises a pied-à-terre for grandparents atop a street-side garage separated from the young owners' house by a central courtyard. Both homes have "inhabitable" skins.

The main house's open
front door is in line with the
kitchen and a door to the
new back patio.

Instead of a mere face-lift, he suggested that to add light throughout the main house they ought to remove the awkward back room to make space for a rear garden and add extra space on the front of the main house to better engage with the courtyard in the middle. To visually unify the addition and the old buildings he proposed a new skin—like 3-D makeup for an actor—that would give the ensemble a fresh, modern identity.

With the dank rear bedroom gone, the two-story, eight-foot extension on the front of the main house barely adds 500 square feet to the formerly 1,700-square-foot house, but it is enough to reorganize the total space into three bedrooms with three baths. In lieu of the rear room, the owners now have an outdoor dining courtyard adjacent to the new

LEFT: In-floor radiant heating is balanced with cross-ventilation for cooling. Glass doors slide open to link the high-ceilinged dining space to the central courtyard.
TOP: In the adjoining kitchen, doors behind blue counter-height chairs lead to a new patio and pizza oven (not visible).

kitchen. The two-story façade facing the central courtyard is entirely glazed and shaded from the sun by powder-coated metal mesh panels fixed to a dynamic sculptural aluminum armature that looks like folded origami.

"It provides privacy as well as an easy connection to the outdoors," Daly said. "We normally consider the boundary between inside and out a definable line of glass or wall to put a door in. In a project like this house, that line is much

LEFT: In the studio atop the garage, Daly installed a practical galley kitchen and cork floors. New leather-covered Gubi chairs surround an heirloom George Nakashima table.
TOP: A fireplace/storage wall screens off the bed. A roof deck can be glimpsed through the slatted skylight.

the lights on inside, they look like giant paper lanterns amid tropical tree bamboo, palms and gunnera.

During the hot summers, the lush garden provides shade and the protective scrim allows windows in both buildings to be left open for energy-saving cross-ventilation. Meanwhile, solar panels hidden on the roof of the main house gather all that Southern California energy for hot water and in-floor radiant heating.

"The design challenge was to allow grandparents, parents and children to use the space freely without encroaching on the privacy of each building," Daly said.

He has achieved that. The studio apartment above the garage is also protected from direct view by its scrim, but it has an interior reorganized to take advantage of the outdoors as well. A balcony at its main level gives Laybourne's parents a chance to lean out and wave at Laybourne and Bekele's two infants playing in the garden, but a new roof deck affords them a private retreat as well.

Laybourne and Bekele's new multigenerational compound, and even their neighborhood close to Abbot Kinney, are symbols of changing lifestyles in the West, where once sharply drawn lines have blurred.

"In 2005, when we did not have children, this diverse socioeconomic area far from the world of television and Hollywood already offered us all the things we thought we needed," Bekele, whose parents are from Ethiopia, said. "It was just great to stroll through the neighborhood to get to stores instead of having to get into a car and on a freeway. Now we realize that when we take a walk, our children also get to see people who look like both their parents." □

thicker and the boundary between inside and out is blurred and the skin is also inhabitable space."

A matching aluminum armature to support a perforated cloak with strategic openings for views of the garden also encloses the garage and apartment across the courtyard.

These two sunshades undulate and project into the courtyard, providing private yet convivial opposing balcony spaces for the master bedroom as well as the guest suite. Light filters through the filigreed skin into the loft-like living spaces of the house, which are filled with spare modernist furnishings, including a George Nakashima table Laybourne inherited from his grandmother, Ray and Charles Eames chairs, and new Vegetal chairs by the Bouroullec brothers. The gauzy white powder-coated metal scrims soften the rectilinear structures they protect, and in the evening, with

Los Angeles House, California

MARMOL RADZINER + ASSOCIATES

"There is no such thing as an imperfect building site," architect Ron Radziner, a principal in the Los Angeles firm Marmol Radziner + Associates, said with conviction, and a steep, east-facing hillside lot in the city's Rustic Canyon neighborhood where he designed a house for a couple in the garment business is ample proof.

The site inspired a building that seems to step up the hill like a mountain climber, and it also merges into the landscape in a way that the original, awkwardly high, two-story house that used to stand in the rear of the wooded, wedge-shaped site did not.

FACING AND RIGHT: At the top of a curved driveway, burnished concrete block basements contain a garage and, on the left, an office under the guest cottage.

ABOVE: Concrete and wood stairs go up the hill to a glass bridge that connects living spaces and bedrooms.

"With this building we wanted to connect to the landscape," Radziner said. "We wanted to be rooted in it and also free from it."

The new house perched halfway up the hill site is made up of three small buildings that are partially sunken into the hillside. They are deftly linked together by steps, decks and a covered bridge to encompass more than 4,000 square feet of space, and yet they look like a set of single-story cottages disappearing into the woods.

To contend with the steep slope, "We placed two square concrete footings halfway up the hill and two rectangular foundations up higher," Radziner explained.

The separate foundations support the three-pavilion structure comprising single-story as well as double-story sections. The larger pavilions are linked by a glass-walled bridge,

and the courtyard spaces between them form private outdoor rooms with a shallow, narrow pool to reflect the sky.

Creating sheltered spaces like these have become second nature for Radziner, whose clients include paparazzi-shy Hollywood celebrities such as Tom Ford and Demi Moore.

"Our goal was to provide guests their own space and to position a guesthouse in a way that they would not intrude into the couple's interior courtyard," Radziner said.

The smallest building, a cube-like pavilion halfway up the hill, houses a studio and a guest suite above it that is cantilevered and wedged partially into the hillside. It has no windows looking into the courtyard behind it, but "guests have a view of the street and oaks and pines on the property," Radziner said. "And from some angles you can't tell where its green roof ends and where the garden begins." The roof garden is ingeniously irrigated by water from a natural pond on the site that is fed by runoff from the house as well as an underground river, which obviates the need for a circulation pump or filter for the pond.

Adjacent to the studio on its right, a two-car garage at the end of a driveway forms the base for part of the northside pavilion on top of the hill that contains living and dining spaces. Across the central courtyard, the third pavilion, set back slightly from the other buildings and canted out to parallel the lot line, is also partially embedded in the ground. It contains the master suite and an extra bedroom.

"From the street you can see the studio and guesthouse building has two stories, but from the neighbors' perspective it sits a whole story lower than the old home," Radziner said.

At the highest, flattest and widest point of the lot where the old house used to be, Radziner installed a 75-foot lap pool on a north-south axis. "The owner loves to swim and

LEFT: The living pavilion, the glass bridge in the middle and a canted bedroom wing (also seen above) form a secret dappled trapezoidal courtyard with a lap pool.

this was his only specific requirement besides privacy and light," the architect recalled.

The structure's burnished concrete blocks, galvanized steel paneling and large expanses of glass, which have become Marmol Radziner's stock-in-trade, echo the Southern California palette explored by Frank Lloyd Wright, Rudolph Schindler and midcentury Case Study architects. The chiseled, clean-lined buildings are also precursors of unpainted steel, concrete and glass prefabricated buildings developed by the firm's other principal, architect Leo Marmol.

"You could paint concrete block and galvanized metal, but when they age naturally they do look better and that is what we aim for," Radziner said. "Houses soften and patinate with age, and this one will merge into the landscape and look even better in ten years." □

Phoenix Live/Work, Arizona

BLANK STUDIO ARCHITECTURE

"Although this looks like an object building, I designed it to serve very specific needs from the inside out. I am not aiming for modernism with a capital 'M,'" architect Matthew Trzebiatowski said about his first building in Phoenix, a 2,250-square-foot, three-story studio and home he designed for himself on a lot abutting a mountain preserve.

"I moved from Wisconsin to Arizona to be a part of a circle that includes Frank Lloyd Wright and a great school of contemporary architecture," he said.

Now an associate professor at Wright's Taliesin West in Scottsdale, Trzebiatowski was drawn to well-known regional talents such as Will Bruder, Wendell Burnette, Rick Joy and Jack DeBartolo—all linked tangentially to Wright or the school—who have developed a bold, boxy modernism. Their buildings have powerful tectonic shapes, expressive skins of steel, large windows, and indoor/outdoor rooms and courtyards that mesh with the desert landscape.

At his relatively new architectural practice called blank studio, Trzebiatowski has staked out his own ground within that particular circle.

While he adopts the prevalent penchant for desert-proof materials, his reductive, cubist approach has resulted in a taut, sculptural, L-shaped building. At first glance, its corrugated and woven Cor-Ten steel mesh cladding seems at odds with its natural backdrop, but "it is meant to rust naturally to the color of the landscape," Trzebiatowski explained. To underscore that idea he even calls it Xeros, which means "dry" in Greek, "to be mindful of this desert place we are in."

TOP LEFT: Street-side trees provide additional shade.

LEFT: The simply furnished bedroom faces north. A net curtain emulates metal mesh screens outside that shade the building.

FACING: The cantilevered bedroom has a large window wall.

"Oxidized steel has been done in Arizona before, but I have deliberately pushed it to an uncomfortable extreme for my home," he said. In some ways it is a metaphor for Phoenix, because like the city, "the building requires you to enter it before you discover that it is quite comfortable inside."

The 600-square-foot ground floor laid on a south-north axis on its narrow sloping site has a compact eco-conscious footprint. It includes Trzebiatowski's high-ceilinged architecture studio, which has a $3\frac{1}{2}$-foot-wide by $19\frac{1}{2}$-foot-tall

LEFT: The green bedroom balcony seen through metal scrims.
BOTTOM LEFT: The front door opens in a grooved track.
BELOW: The elegant front stairs to the architect's home.
FACING: Open-plan living spaces lead to the bedroom.
OVERLEAF: The studio courtyard and $19\frac{1}{2}$-foot-tall front door.

ABOVE: A curved Corbusier-esque steel staircase leads to a mezzanine gallery in the compact studio. FACING: Models of built and unbuilt projects displayed upstairs. Cor-Ten scrims attached to the façade soften sunlight that pours in.

steel and glass hinged front door and a mezzanine that overlooks the central space. The 1,000-square-foot top floor, where the architect lives with his wife and toddler son, has an open-plan living space and a hallway that links it to a master suite and nursery in back. It is cantilevered above the lower double-height studio like a hammerhead crane, terminating in an "L" shape. A full wall of glass in the master bedroom faces north toward the hills, and on the other side a yellow glass–framed "Romeo and Juliet" viewing balcony— a nod to Bauhaus and Le Corbusier—projects outward, facing south-central Phoenix.

Solid steel panels clad the west wall of the building to keep the sun out. The east and south sides have woven steel scrims that cast dappled shadows on the structure and help to mitigate the intensity of the unrelenting morning sun.

"There is a decorative quality to the scrim, but beauty was not the goal. It was done for shade. Louvers and broad overhangs can also do that, but here the mesh is a compositional device and it was done for a practical reason," the architect said.

Although Trzebiatowski desired a live/work space, he "wanted to make a studio that was completely separate and a very private home space," offering a clear rationale for the lack of internal circulation between the two.

Visible from the street, a long exterior flight of stairs leads up to a landing/foyer for the living spaces on the top floor. At ground level, hidden from view behind the woven steel scrims, a short flight of steps goes down to a gravel courtyard and the double-height studio door on its east side.

"I open that door and I come in to work. It is a simple but powerful way for the mind to switch gears," the architect said. Inside, a sculptural spiral staircase of steel goes up to Trzebiatowski's mezzanine office. Seen through west-facing glass walls, the woven, handworked quality of the cladding outside also seems artful and helps to counter the harshness of the rectilinear shapes.

"If these spaces were machined too tightly, like an iPod, they would not resonate. I wanted unpredictable features made by hand with inevitable imperfections," Trzebiatowski said, adding, "In a home and studio like ours, things have to feel more elastic."

Engineered wood joists, poured concrete foundation walls and clear or laminated colored glass panels complement the steel palette. Inside, hand-finished concrete floors, wax-sealed white gypsum plaster, clear-sealed oriented strand board ceilings, and dark plum-colored Euroform board or Latvian plywood floors and millwork are all foils for the exposed Cor-Ten steel framing.

In the Wrightian world Trzebiatowski has stepped into, decorative details are not frowned upon, but he prefers to avoid them and tries instead "to get down to essentials." □

San Francisco Condo, California

GARY HUTTON DESIGN

Chara Schreyer, a trustee at the San Francisco Museum of Modern Art and a prominent collector of contemporary art, often describes the varied works displayed in her several Bay Area homes, which include art by Sol LeWitt, Jeff Wall, Richard Serra, Andy Warhol and Fred Sandback, as "many collections within a collection."

Her move into a new San Francisco pied-à-terre in a modern high-rise tower gave her a unique opportunity to invigorate her multifaceted collection—among the most important in the world of modern art—with a bespoke gallery that is itself a work of art.

LEFT: In the gallery-like setting, Ed Ruscha's canvas *Etc.* dominates dinner conversations. Space-saving pole lamps by Venini adjoin tailored, upholstered sofas by Hutton.
BELOW: A gallery/hallway leads to the master suite.

"I just happened to become a collector. I didn't plan it," Schreyer said about the collection that grew spontaneously ever since she was at UC Berkeley studying art history. However, the gallery, a 2,700-square-foot condominium with gleaming white epoxy floors and crisp white walls, is no accident.

The daughter of a Southern California developer, Schreyer has a nose for real estate, and she signed on as a prospective buyer before the Four Seasons building designed by Del Campo & Maru Architects had even broken ground. As soon as the building was ready, the modernist collector arrived with San Francisco interior designer Gary Hutton and chose an odd trapezoidal apartment on the 24th floor—with a prominent view of the Humboldt Bank Building's opulent beaux arts dome.

"It's a conversation. And you change the meaning of things when they are juxtaposed against such opposites," Schreyer said.

Usually, juxtaposing dissimilar art in her collection to promote dialogue is enough, but here, with her plan to show works such as Ed Ruscha's painting *Etc.* in the dining room

FACING AND RIGHT: Hutton's square tables can be joined; comfortable Brno armchairs are by Knoll. In the background, near Richard Artschwager's *Prototype for Exclamation Point*, pivot doors lead to an office that doubles as the guest room.

RIGHT, TOP: Architect Tim Gemmill rearranged the kitchen and powder room within a white cube in the open-plan living, dining and gallery space. On the gallery wall between those rooms is a circular drawing by Richard Serra. In the background, near a Dodo chair by Cassina, a white piloti camouflages old plumbing pipes.

OVERLEAF, LEFT: In the artful powder room, a fiber-optic frame surrounds the mirror in which Robert Gober's *Hanging Man/ Sleeping Man* wallpaper is reflected. The steel toilet paper rack is by Gemmill. The doors become obscure when locked.

OVERLEAF, RIGHT: Larry Bell's *Untitled* sculpture in the gallery.

alongside other equally ambiguous or feisty word-related works, an outré provocation became vital.

Hutton invited architect Tim Gemmill to transform the three-bedroom condominium, which had only a tiny hallway and few display walls, into an urban oasis for art.

"It all had to come down. Chara's collection needed open space, and that's true of modern art in general," Gemmill said, reiterating his design maxim.

He eliminated one bedroom (a real estate no-no), with some resistance from Schreyer, created a master suite at one end, and rearranged the rest of the space as open-plan living, dining and gallery rooms that flow around an enclosed core containing a compact state-of-the-art kitchen and a powder room with a partition made of steel and toilet paper rolls.

Visitors lucky enough to be invited in can now circumambulate Gemmill's white "box within a box" cube in the middle of the gallery.

Hutton and Gemmill worked meticulously to save the all-white gallery from becoming monotonous by adding a few more elegant and surprising touches for aficionados to enjoy. Where walls meet floors and ceilings, Gemmill's card-thin reveals are obsessively perfect. Hutton enlivened the powder room with an artful paper-roll tower, fiber-optic lights and a see-through door that gets cloudy when it is locked from inside. Finally, they stretched fabric across the ceilings throughout the apartment to absorb any distracting ambient sounds that could take away from the perfect, monastic silence of the collection talking. □

San Francisco Live/Work, California

INTERSTICE ARCHITECTS

Architect Andrew Dunbar and his wife, landscape architect Zoee Astrakhan, both principals in the firm Interstice Architects, bought a derelict 1908 Edwardian in San Francisco's dense Mission District because it was all they could afford, but they transformed it over several years with resourceful, elegant and rich ideas that belie the off-the-shelf and recycled materials they used. The house incorporates their 1,100-square-foot home upstairs and an art gallery below, as well as their firm's offices. The renovated building showcases many aspects of the couple's creative mettle.

"The house is where we experiment," Dunbar said. "We weren't so much trying to do 'green' things as just wanting to be able to live in a better way."

When they first moved in, they literally camped out in their gutted house, cooking on a portable stove and sleeping in a pitched tent. They observed sunlight streaming in from southeast-facing windows in the rear, and envisioned the potential of solar panels and a protected herb garden on different sections of the roof.

"We tried to imagine a home where we would also exercise our interest in edible landscaping and the use of gray water," Astrakhan said. Dunbar's taste for affordable recycled building materials aligns with her thinking, and he realized that there was a lot they could make together by hand. "We both learned to build and to weld so we could fashion what we needed," Dunbar said. As they embarked on a

LEFT: A custom wood-and-aluminum Dutch door to an office and gallery on the ground floor adds warmth to a reflective façade of salvaged double-paned windows carefully fitted like regular wood or slate shingles onto horizontal steel ribs.
FACING: Original Edwardian bays above the gallery.

ABOVE AND FACING: The open living area allows for a roomy IKEA kitchen island with custom details. Stairs go to the roof. LEFT: The children's room and a green-walled master suite. OVERLEAF: The central blue bathroom has glass mosaic floors, acrylic wall panels and a retractable roof. A door near the dining table slides open for access to the back spiral stairs. The Hans Wegner chairs are heirlooms.

series of do-it-yourself projects to save money, they found unexpected and extremely satisfying design solutions.

It soon became clear that "we could make an open-plan house more energy efficient," Dunbar said.

Dunbar is French Canadian and Astrakhan is from New Hampshire, so they both understood that compared to northeastern cities San Francisco enjoys a relatively

TOP: The new prefab roof deck with boxed beds for a kitchen garden also has ipe benches and a hot tub powered by solar panels that are visible on the older, sloped section of the roof. ABOVE AND FACING: The plastic rear wall inside and out.

perpetual summer. Instead of adding an expensive gas or radiant heating system that would see little use, they covered the sunny rear wall in translucent plastic panels commonly used for greenhouse roofs.

The inexpensive corrugated thermal plastic sheathing attached to each side of the two-story wall studs radiates heat during winter when the sun is low and shines directly on it. On days when it gets too hot, sections of the translucent wall that hang on overhead tracks can be slid open to cool the interior.

The house has no windows along its sides, so to bring natural light and air into its center, Dunbar cut a wide slot into the roof above the centrally located bathroom and added a giant retractable skylight. The walls are covered with back-painted cast acrylic plastic tiles that are water- and mold-resistant and easily shed any rain that falls in. The mosaic-tiled floor, an attractive counterpoint, slopes imperceptibly toward a drain in the center.

The owners' proudest moment was the installation of a glass façade and a double Dutch front door to the front gallery. This street-level, storefront window treatment is completely original. Reclaimed, double-insulated glass sheets for windows of varying widths and sizes are arranged like shingles on horizontal strips of steel welded to the structural moment frame. Gaps between the shingles are caulked to keep the weather out. Each reclaimed pane varies slightly in color, so when the sun shines into the gallery during the late afternoon, painterly patches of colored light fall on the concrete floor. "We didn't anticipate that," Dunbar said, pleased.

One maxim the designers now espouse emerged with the birth of their two daughters: "Always design multipurpose, flexible spaces," Astrakhan said. Thus tough steel floors in their home office allow the children to ride tricycles in from the garden, and a luminous plastic potting shed doubles as a dollhouse. The couple's elastic approach is useful in dense cities. "We've learned that when you do it right," Dunbar said, "1,100 square feet of living space is not small." □

San Francisco Loft, California
FOUGERON ARCHITECTURE

"Light and transparency feature frequently in my work," San Francisco architect Anne Fougeron said. Her freestanding, channel glass–walled buildings in Silicon Valley and a retreat for a family in Big Sur near the central California coast are good examples of buildings she has designed that are prisms to refract light into the interior.

However, in San Francisco's SOMA District, for a two-story 1930s concrete structure with large north-facing windows that is hemmed in between similar buildings on its east, west and south sides, glass walls were not an option.

Since the best light source was directly above the building, skylights to illuminate the interior seemed to be the best

FACING: The steel Grasshopper cap is just high enough to accommodate a mezzanine bedroom.
ABOVE: The hemmed-in 1930s warehouse building has an office and garage below the duplex loft Fougeron designed.

solution. However, Fougeron and project manager Todd Aranaz decided to cut two large holes in the roof. Over one they designed a sculptural steel and glass cap that seems like a giant translucent insect hovering over the roof. The other, a 16-foot square hole directly above a glass-walled enclosure on the main floor, opens the loft to light and air. "We created a real courtyard with rocks and grass inside the enclosure," Fougeron said.

Fougeron was educated in France but received her degree in architecture from UC Berkeley at a time when influential Bay Area architect Joe Esherick of Sea Ranch fame was at

ABOVE: The bedroom loft with a see-through glass bathroom has showy views of downtown San Francisco.
FACING: A trapezoidal door opens to the roof deck. White, all-weather ottomans from DZINE are by Konstantin Grcic.

the helm of the Architecture Department at the College of Environmental Design. Green thinking was taken very seriously. She represents an avant-garde generation of Bay Area architects who endeavor to integrate spare, modern structures with their natural environment, and the courtyard notion she developed grew out of her clients Jason Shelton and Amy Shimer's desire for an indoor/outdoor setting in the heart of a crowded, industrial neighborhood. Even the insect-like skylight design—Fougeron's first structure with

canted glass walls, and reminiscent of Austrian architects Coop Himmelb(l)au's whimsical 1988 locust-like rooftop office for a Viennese law firm—actually grew out of a rational need for more space.

"My clients had talked about adding a penthouse at first, but when that was not feasible we thought of cutting a large hole in between the wooden roof joists and capping it to provide headroom for a new third-floor master bedroom mezzanine," Fougeron said. "To bring as much visual interest as possible I looked at structures that have funky geometries like enclosures for staircases that go up to roofs. We made ours like a grasshopper shape with its legs sticking out."

The see-through lid, ingeniously composed of affordable fixed steel window systems attached to a steel armature, throws light into the entire 14-foot-high main level that is built above a ground-floor office. At the same time, the insulated, low-E glass top provides passive solar heat and dramatically spotlights a sculptural new steel staircase that connects the main level to the mezzanine.

Strategically positioned on the north side of the roof, the so-called Grasshopper does not cast its own shadow into the new courtyard below. Sunlight streams all day directly into the second-floor atrium and filters unobstructedly into virtually every corner of the loft, because sliding partitions that divide spaces around the central atrium like conventional rooms in a house are also all made of clear glass—as requested by Shelton and Shimer.

"Most loft rooms are very dark and never have such natural light," Fougeron said. Although the clear glass walls provide little visual privacy, they do make the rooms ranged around the courtyard seem bigger and poetically ephemeral.

The more practical aspects of the design include a trapezoidal exit from the Grasshopper mezzanine that allows cross-ventilation and rooftop access; Cor-Ten steel exterior cladding and an ipe wood roof deck that are both weather resistant and self-sealing; and dimmable T5 fluorescent tubes for night lighting, which save a lot of energy.

BELOW: A dining arrangement next to the fireplace near the front windows. RIGHT: In the living room, the coffee table is by George Nelson. To counter the loft's industrial look, the open atrium has real turf and river rocks.

Although Fougeron admires Japanese architects such as Ryue Nishizawa, whose unusual buildings sometimes emulate natural forms literally, her green building—despite its canted glass Grasshopper—has strict straight lines.

"Recently the curved line is everywhere. It is not better or worse," Fougeron said. "On the West Coast, where buildings share a design language left over from Case Study mid-century buildings, curved lines seem out of context. They just don't seem natural." □

Seattle Condo, Washington

TERRY HUNZIKER INC.

Interior designer Terry Hunziker's childhood in blue-collar Longview, a small lumber town in Washington State, resurfaces in his penchant for wood and bark details in his work, which is best described as modern.

"But I don't adhere to ultramodernist rules," the designer said. "I use a lot of soft, warm materials to determine how a space will feel, not how it will look."

His high-ceilinged contemporary condominium in Seattle, an ongoing experiment to show clients the full range

ABOVE: The luxurious terrace off the master suite provides a leafy garden space amid gritty Seattle high-rises.
RIGHT: Hunziker's eclectic den on the new east end has built-ins, a 1915 Thonet armchair and a white sculpture by Peter Millett.

of such a neutral, natural palette that also includes embedded runners of patinated cold-rolled steel to suggest hallways or rooms in its open plan, is within a refurbished four-story 1898 brick building that used to be a hotel. Hunziker's condo comprises three adjacent duplexes cleverly conjoined over a period of 15 years to form the carefully composed two-level home he shares with his two dogs.

"I don't like seeing everything at once. I need levels, I need to go around corners and partitions to see things that are not readily apparent," the designer explained. "I need a variety of experiences."

The most recent addition enlarges the condo to a total of 2,900 square feet. A 900-square-foot terrace on the top floor faces downtown and the Olympic Mountains, adding to the feeling of an urban nature retreat. It is also an elegant showcase for art and sculptural objects, including furniture Hunziker has designed. Japanese-style joinery and heavy timber have long been associated with a regional Pacific Northwest look, but in Hunziker's hands such details, used more delicately, echo the work of some of his heroes such as 1930s French designers Jean-Michel Frank and Jean Prouvé. Indeed, the latter's dictum, "logic, balance and purity" of form, seems to have become Hunziker's own.

Hunziker's palette of mossy greens, tertiary colors and natural materials, and his deep interest in early twentieth-century design as well as crafts from Europe, Africa and Asia, actually evolved when he worked with celebrated Seattle interior designer Jean Jongeward, who died in 2000.

"She was my mentor," Hunziker said, discounting his own training as an artist. "I learned hands on from her and that was my education."

TOP: The dining area next to a floating red plaster partition has circa 1815 Russian chairs. LEFT: A chair prototype by Alvar Aalto sits in the foyer. On the stair wall is a round canvas by Ken Kelly. FACING: Art by Anne Appleby on a wall covered with car paint. OVERLEAF: Hunziker's *objets* in artful vignettes.

LEFT: The bedroom has views of the terrace through its gallery hallway. BOTTOM: A scrap-metal screen by David Gulassa and an old settee mesh with Hunziker's chairs. FACING: Fitted carpeting abuts dark steel floors.

In time he developed new architectural and design strategies of his own. Freestanding walls such as a Venetian red partition in the entry that veils the dining area directly behind it, floor-to-ceiling steel and translucent glass pocket doors that disappear like shoji screens when not needed, and thin reveals between walls, ceilings and floors that do meet are some details that typify Hunziker's distinctive look.

Other tricks he uses in his own home recur in rooms for clients. "The north window wall was just a flat brick wall," he said. "I built it out between each window so it would have some depth, and I replaced the transom windows and their casings with French doors." As a result, the inset windows appear narrower and taller than they are and create a modern loggia effect. Metal ceiling panels recall Victorian-era tin ceilings, and in the absence of interior walls and doors, different types of flooring signal transitions between spaces just as painted floors do in Gerrit Rietveld's Schröder House.

"I consciously switched floor materials from one area to the next. Even your bare feet should know where you are," he said. For instance, the living room has wood floors but the new kitchen has floors made of waxed steel. Sisal carpeting makes it easy for the dogs to go up a flight of stairs that leads up to the master bedroom suite, which opens to the terrace formed by a city-required setback from the street.

"Upstairs I have a different kind of art gallery with a garden and city view," Hunziker said, pointing to a lush container garden where he likes to entertain. It is as close to the country as he would like to be.

"Although I talk about natural colors, I am not a country boy," he said emphatically. "I like living in the city. When I step out into busy Pioneer Square I can be among people whenever I want." □

Studio.bna's Wapiti Valley prairie home in Wyoming.

Desert/Prairie

Anchorage House, Alaska

MAYER SATTLER-SMITH

As soon as Martin Buser, one of Alaska's most distinguished long-distance mushers and an Iditarod dog-sledding champion, spotted the work of Anchorage-based Klaus Mayer and Petra Sattler-Smith in an architecture magazine he wanted them to design a home for him and his wife, Kathy, on 20 scenic acres of woodlands they owned near Anchorage.

Swiss-born Buser is a former horticulturist, and he may have sensed that Mayer and Sattler-Smith, who are both German, are also avid environmentalists. They view contemporary architecture, interior design and furniture through the twin lenses of practicality and resource conservation.

FACING: The charred spruce-clad building is a lens through which to view the landscape. RIGHT: The site comprises a glacial hill surrounded by woodlands. BELOW: Martin Buser takes his huskies for an outing.

"They had incorporated the site into their design and it seemed like a minimal intrusion on the land," Buser recalled. He also liked their cubist, contemporary aesthetic, which veered away from typical log cabin or gabled Tudor clichés.

"We look to connect the spirit of this place to modern architecture that frames the landscape but also helps to conserve it, " Mayer said.

Alaska's historical Russian trappers, fur traders and itinerant nineteenth-century gold miners were also thinking about natural resources, but obviously from a different perspective. When they settled there, they retreated to conservative values, and everything, including architecture, that worked in their past was repeated in "a straightforward,

no-nonsense, needs-to-work way," Mayer said. The impact this had on their surroundings was not considered. "Even today there is not an expression of this culture and place in buildings that are contemporary. We wanted to change that," Mayer added.

So the musher's new award-winning 2,450-square-foot, flat-top home on a moraine hill surrounded by lakes, woods and meadows formed by forest fires is a poster child for Mayer Sattler-Smith's thinking.

TOP: The house shelters a courtyard that has one spruce tree. The central foyer doubles as a practical mudroom.
FACING: The interior is aimed at views of Mount McKinley.

LEFT: A cinder-block fireplace dominates the cedar-clad interior.
ABOVE: The front deck is also a prospect for Buser's pets.

The principal materials of the boxy structure that Buser built by hand—concrete blocks for retaining walls outside and poured floors inside, native spruce for exterior siding and fragrant yellow cedar for interior cladding—all come from the area. Its low, hunkered-down "L" shape forms a courtyard protected from the wind, while its large and small glass windows frame views of the Alaskan mountain ranges. The winding driveway leads conveniently to a changing room for the musher before he enters his home.

"The house is a refuge and a prospect, a point of departure and return," Mayer said.

The central open-plan living space is long and narrow, like a squared telescope with Mount McKinley, North

FACING: The kitchen/dining area with cedar wood-lined walls and ceilings has Alvar Aalto Model 611 chairs. The owners also collect artifacts such as the Eskimo sculpture on the table.
RIGHT: The foyer mudroom with tall windows for pets to look out jogs into living spaces that have easy-care concrete floors.
RIGHT, BOTTOM: A view of the Zen entry courtyard.

America's tallest peak, in its sights. Strategic wall openings on each side frame views of the Chugach Mountains and Mount Susitna, and the bedroom wing facing west has different views of the mountains.

A few furnishings complement seating that keeps the interior clutter free, but also provide "comfortable places to sit and look at the main attractions outside," Buser said. "Some windows come low to the ground so that even our pets can look out."

A heat-recovery ventilation system, triple-pane glazing and double-firred exterior walls are invisible but crucial energy-saving features during the coldest months. Paradoxically, during the summer, temperatures rise dramatically and wildfires fanned by high winds claim swaths of trees. Aware that embers from such fires could scar the house, the architects recommended a traditional Japanese blowtorched finish for the unpainted siding. The blackened crust is maintenance free. It helps the house blend into the landscape and "is also a passive solar heat collector," Sattler-Smith said.

The fire-resistant concrete courtyard is ideal for outdoor living year-round. Whether temperatures rise or fall, it is a comfortable spot with a heated pool that doubles as a fire-fighting reservoir. Sheltered from the wind and sun, it has Zen elements such as a trickling water fountain, a fire pit for cooking and an iconic black spruce tree relocated from the meadow below. A roof terrace, yet another intimate refuge, is the place to watch aurora borealis shows in the night skies.

From its vantage point the house overlooks woodlands and rolling meadows where the owners' huskies run and where "we first taught both our boys how to ski," Buser said. "This land was home long before we built this house on it." □

Palm Springs House, California

MARMOL RADZINER PREFAB

"My wife, Alisa Becket, and I find the quality of light and the color of the desert landscape irresistible," said Los Angeles architect Leo Marmol, who has built himself a modular twenty-first-century vacation home on five acres in Desert Hot Springs, California, minutes away from Palm Springs and two hours away from their home in Santa Monica.

"We like being near the Pacific, but this land that we've been coming to with both our children for several years has a view of San Jacinto Peak and the mountains that form this valley. It is powerful and peaceful at the same time."

Their Desert Home, composed of ten of the first steel-frame indoor/outdoor dwelling modules to leave Marmol Radziner's prefabrication factory in Vernon, California, arrived on trailers. The construction barely disturbed the

LEFT: A covered deck frames San Jacinto Peak and connects the master wing, on the left, to the office and guest wing.
ABOVE: Two modules meet; a glimpse of the guest wing.

FACING: A cactus garden abuts the master wing; sliding glass doors on two sides open to decks and the courtyard pool.
ABOVE: Floating concrete steps lead to the front door.

soil because modules were craned into place over concrete block foundations within a little over a week's time.

Its lavish L-plan arrangement, with wood-and-glass-walled rooms, loggias and decks that face views of the painterly desert or look onto a sheltered courtyard with a swimming pool and fire pit, and the high-end appliances, wooden cabinets and polished concrete floors within its 2,000-square-foot interior, belie prefab's cash-conscious and ugly-looks reputation. In spirit, Marmol's two-bedroom, two-bath prototypal home, which includes a separate guest wing and studio and 3,000 square feet of covered and open decks, clearly take its cues from architect Richard Neutra's finely detailed historic 1940s Kaufmann Desert House in nearby Palm Springs that Marmol's firm, Marmol Radziner + Associates restored during the 1990s.

"There is no major advantage in making a prefab building just to make an inexpensive home," Marmol said. "When you have a remote site in the desert without a construction infrastructure, prefab is the only way to make even a higher-end modern structure feasible. That's why we did it."

A lack of infrastructure was precisely why prefabricated buildings arrived in California during the gold rush of 1849,

when low-cost dwellings that could be quickly assembled were shipped in from industrial England. However, they were soon abandoned. Whenever low-end, affordable kit homes—like postwar veterans housing—reappeared on the Pacific Coast, they gave way to nobler experiments. Bucky Fuller's utopian 1950s geodesic domes, which cropped up as tony California hippie retreats, and the midcentury Case Study houses such as Ray and Charles Eames's home in Pacific Palisades, which is made of mass-produced off-the-shelf components, are still elegant, relevant and influential.

Although early twenty-first-century enthusiasm for pre-fabricated buildings has slackened, "Prefab will be back because it also ties into ideas of sustainability," Marmol said.

LEFT: The sheltered courtyard next to a swimming pool has an oxidized steel fire pit and benches made of recycled lumber.
BELOW: Views of the guest pavilion from the living room. Marmol's wife, designer Alisa Becket, accessorized furniture by Marmol Radziner, indoors and out.

The Desert House demonstrates those ideas amply. The large doors and windows all have triple-pane, low-E, argon-filled insulating glass. Solar panels located on the roof above the bedroom module provide power. Deep overhangs provide shade during the summer, while window shades pocketed into the ceilings provide more protection from the sun.

"In the winter, the concrete floors absorb the sun's heat and stay warm all night long," Marmol said.

There are other benefits. The factory-made modules are made of recycled steel rather than nonsustainable wood framing, and since most of the building materials are cut at the Marmol Radziner factory, there is little waste. Excess material simply gets reused to make smaller components. "At the factory, we can almost build everything—the modules, landscape features, interiors, furnishings—and make a complete environment," Marmol said. "Combining more than one module can be as creative a process as designing a custom house. The only limitation is working within fixed dimensional parameters for trucking them on highways."

However, like other modernists since the Industrial Revolution who tried to deliver high design at less cost, Marmol Radziner also discovered that fine detailing gets expensive. "Even Case Study houses failed to curb costs. But with factory developments and efficiencies, prefab housing does come closer to achieving that goal," Marmol said.

Becket's grandfather was the modernist architect Welton Becket, who left his indelible stamp on Los Angeles with buildings such as the Cinerama Dome (inspired by Bucky Fuller's geodesic domes). She worked on the interior design, incorporating furniture designed by Marmol and adding painterly touches that help meld the building into its setting.

Becket's choices of vintage, contemporary and custom pieces in tertiary colors were inspired by the desert. "Her design, like the indoor/outdoor architecture, responds to the site," Marmol said. "Our goal was to have it all fit together so well so that you don't for a moment think that this modern home was prefabricated." □

FACING: Poured concrete floors inside and out make poolside living easy. The kitchen cabinetry is by Marmol Radziner.
TOP AND ABOVE: Living spaces and a master bedroom all open to a common deck facing the pool.

Scottsdale House, Arizona

MICHAEL P. JOHNSON DESIGN STUDIO

From his teacher's pulpit at Frank Lloyd Wright's Taliesin West, which is a celebrated architectural school and the repository of Wright's archive in Scottsdale, Arizona, Michael P. Johnson, an unlicensed architect from Milwaukee, has expounded his modernist views for three decades on how—and when—to build in such desert areas, where summer temperatures exceed 120 degrees in the shade.

To avoid the sun, "I just habitually work early," he said in a voice made stentorian and gravelly by whiskey, smoking and the dry desert air.

Occasionally he invites his best students to produce working drawings at the eponymous design studio he shares with his wife in Cave Creek, just an hour north of Scottsdale.

One such project, on the drawing boards only a few years ago, is now the modern home of Treg Bradley, founder of American Agritech, a hydroponics company that markets products for growing orchids "and other plants," Johnson said with a chuckle. Bradley also invented the Grobal, a self-watering houseplant pot designed by New York industrial designer Karim Rashid.

"Treg found me about ten years ago because of my reputation in the Phoenix area. I looked at his two-and-a-half-acre property in North Scottsdale, and it wasn't until he got divorced a few years later that he contacted me again to design this home," Johnson said.

Bradley lives alone now, entertains frequently and collects clothes, cars and art. Having grown up in a Robert

LEFT: A view of the house balanced atop a hump in the land. Its bedroom wings cantilever on each side of the living spaces, well above undisturbed terrain.
OVERLEAF: The front gate; living spaces are aligned with a central swimming pool that is directly opposite the front door.

Frankeberger–designed home in Gilbert, Bradley was keen on a modern design, even though his list of requirements—a four-car garage, a master bedroom with an enormous closet, his and her bathrooms and two guest bedrooms for friends—could just as easily have been interpreted as a suburban Tuscan-style villa. However, he needed a home to showcase his sizeable collection of expressionistic art by local talents such as Hector Ruiz and Colin Chillag, and vintage Italian furniture from the 1970s.

"The paintings are for the most part bold, contemporary and big," Johnson said, and they also determined the aesthetic and layout of the house. "Although the main interior space was to be open in plan, I knew there would have to be many long, white gallery walls for art."

Finally, the slender, bar-shaped, stucco-clad, single-story home that took shape was built with floor-to-ceiling tinted glass on its north and south sides that face rolling desert landscapes that are part of a nature conservation area.

The house stretches from east to west and looks south toward "a sentinel of stone," Johnson said. "So I focused the central living room on that natural landmark. It made sense to set the living and dining rooms and kitchen atop a hump of land and to float the two bedroom wings on each side above the desert so we wouldn't disturb soil underneath."

As a result, only about half of the elongated 4,400-square-foot house is built directly on the ground. Promenades parallel to the house lead from the garage on the east side and from the sculptural red front gate on the west to the front door precisely in the center of the north façade.

"You enter the living, dining and kitchen areas, and the smoked-glass sliding doors before you make the house seem transparent. You just see the desert," Johnson said.

For Bradley, who is an avid naturalist, that is the most impressive painting he could ever buy.

"That's why, except for some decorative native plantings along the promenade, we didn't change any of the environment around the house," Johnson said.

A narrow, 185-foot back deck, from where Bradley can also take in the view, is shared by both the bedroom wings. The indoor/outdoor aspect allows for natural ventilation, and the deck, linked to a spa and infinity pool in back, seems to merge into the desert.

"I tell my students that you don't need to be an architect to design architecture," Johnson, ever the maverick designer, said. "It is easy. You take the program and then the site tells you to make a building straight or curvilinear or triangular. Not pure whim."

Johnson's own dialogue with the site has resulted in a building that sits well on it.

"In any setting, a new building has to respond to what came before. A commercial building in Phoenix would be different from one in San Francisco," Johnson said, recalling Mies van der Rohe's many preliminary models of the Seagram skyscraper in New York that was built next to Neoclassical neighbors.

"In the end, Mies's black glass building literally reflects the context," Johnson said. "You obviously have more freedom in the desert than he had, but still you have to try not to intrude on the land. I don't believe this house reflects the desert, but it respects it." □

Tundra Outpost, Idaho

OLSON KUNDIG ARCHITECTS

Award-winning Seattle architect Tom Kundig, an avid mountain climber accustomed to pulleys and ropes, has made wheels and pivoting planes an integral aspect of his architectural repertoire. However, for artist and designer Jan Cox he has designed a house and studio/workshop in the high desert of central Idaho whose walls literally stretch out to envelop a paradise garden.

"It's a special, idiosyncratic house," Kundig, a principal at Olson Kundig Architects, said about this still, gestural version of his usually kinetic oeuvre. "A lot of my architecture is contextual," he explains. A simple, hunkered-down outpost in an overwhelming landscape ringed by mountains was the best strategy. "The building had to be hard outside and soft inside," he said.

At first, Cox, who is the daughter of an architect, had considered designing the house herself. "Then I met Tom 10 years ago, and we started work on several different plans,"

LEFT AND ABOVE: Tom Kundig's live/work desert retreat for artist Jan Cox includes a walled paradise garden.
OVERLEAF: Windows above the entry stairs air out the kitchen; cross-shaped windows overlook the garden and fruit trees.

she said, little knowing it would take nearly a decade to iron out all the complications of building in the middle of a lava desert on 20 pristine acres that abut protected grazing acreage. Time, and the rising cost of construction, helped pare the 3,500-square-foot design down to essentials.

The box-like house Kundig devised has within its bar-shaped footprint a square courtyard and a narrow garden—twice as long as the house—contained within 11-foot-high walls made of tough all-weather concrete blocks. On the main floor of the three-story steel frame and concrete block home, a single open-plan space contains the kitchen, living and dining areas. A narrow staircase leads up to a 600-square-foot bedroom and bathroom held aloft by an exposed steel beam. Another staircase goes down to basement rooms and a two-car garage that doubles as a workshop. Windows, some as large as 8 by 11 feet, open the fortified structure on all four sides to the desert so that Cox and her visitors can be spectators in its seasonal pageant of extremes.

"I grew up in the landscape around eastern Washington and near Sun Valley, Idaho," Kundig said. "I know this land. There are two ways of working in landscapes like this and one is not pretending that it ever disappears," he said.

And Cox didn't want it to. The scorching winds, blankets of snow and, in the summer, roaming herds of deer, elk and antelope have been endlessly fascinating for her since the 1970s, when she moved from a waterfront home in Sausalito, California, to be with her husband at the time in Sun Valley, near Ketchum, Idaho. Soon after, she was gifted 20 acres of farmland by her father, and she began to go down from the middle of ski country to show friends the open tundra. "We used to hike in and I would have a long

FACING: The main floor above the garage and office has a compact mezzanine bedroom above the kitchen.
RIGHT, TOP AND BOTTOM: The central fir stairs with sisal carpeting lead to the entry courtyard and long paradise garden.
OVERLEAF: The dining area has a small side deck.

FACING: From the kitchen, grandstand views of mountains.
RIGHT, TOP: A counter divides the kitchen from the dining area.
BOTTOM: A cinder-block fireplace anchors the living room.

picnic table out in the field. That was when I got to study the land. It is very peaceful with wildflowers and sagebrush, and unusual without trees around. One of the goals was to not mess that up," Cox said.

Kundig concurs. "That's why the house is close to the building limit. Even if we were allowed to do a skyscraper it is what we wanted—to hover over the landscape."

The interior developed in a similar collaborative way. "Tom and I were in sync about using only a few materials and no temporary finishes," Cox said. "I wanted things to age in place." So the kitchen counters are of Carrara marble, ceilings are of new fir, some walls are clad in recycled barnwood and the rest with plaster from American Clay. Most of the steel railings and fittings were crafted on-site. Cox, a versatile artist who likes to work with found objects, video and photography, decided to add gradually to pieces and artwork from her father that includes a few Matisses and paintings by friends. The palette is tertiary because, "I am drawn to the landscape. I was also a goldsmithing apprentice, and I bring all I know into interior installations, too," Cox said.

She also decided to cultivate a garden without encroaching on land where coyotes, wolves and deer have free rein. "I knew it was going to be a walled garden. I had conceptualized it for the climate and the wildlife," Cox recalls.

"Tom referred to it as 'a paradise garden' and I had never heard the term," she said, still incredulous. Soon after, she started to read about Islamic paradise gardens and learned that the word "paradise" comes from ancient Persian words for "walled garden." "My house and garden evolved along those lines," she said. "I had planned to grow fruit trees, vegetables, grapes and roses in the desert like the ancients did. My land is exactly like that of those gardens of antiquity where the desert and mountains meet." □

Wapiti Valley House, Wyoming

STUDIO.BNA

"They were not pretending to be cowboys on the weekend. They just love the West," Brett Nave said about a Los Angeles couple that came to his firm looking to build a vacation home on many acres of virgin Wyoming prairie straight out of an old Hollywood Western.

On this pristine land in Wapiti Valley, bordered by craggy mountains near Yellowstone National Park, Nave, a principal at Studio.bna in Montana, designed a new kind of sustainable steel and glass ranch house that is edgy but respectful of its site.

"I did not want to disturb what was there. Sometimes the scrubby land seems serene and pastoral and at other

LEFT AND ABOVE: A rammed-earth rear wall forms a spine for the house. Its butterfly roof is held aloft on steel posts.
OVERLEAF: Bedrooms of varied heights on each side are clad with oxidized steel and linked to the house by decks.

times it is so wild you wonder if you can make it back to your car," Nave said. "You can't just show up and drop a building in such a remarkable place."

The design process with his team and a former partner, Lori Ryker, with whom Nave had built a house in Montana, was therefore equally unusual.

Ryker, an author and teacher who lectures on the virtues of green design, and Nave, a student of legendary Alabama architect Samuel Mockbee, clearly understood the need for

LEFT AND BELOW: The open-plan living room has concrete floors and French doors of steel. The thick earth wall emanates stored heat at night when temperatures drop precipitously.

wall they constructed forms the south wall of a long expressionistic bar-shaped building of earth, glass and recycled steel, with undulating butterfly roofs that mimic the rise and fall of distant mountain ridges. The main house has bedrooms at each end of a central living and dining area, and is connected by decks to guest and office pavilions on the east side. The two-foot-thick rammed-earth wall keeps out the sun's heat and also insulates the 3,100-square-foot home from temperatures that fall well below freezing during the winter. A core of rigid insulation magnifies the wall's insulating capabilities. Composite recycled wood wall panels inside make the house even more earth-friendly.

A north-facing wall of fixed and operable glass panels is a delicate counterpoint to the heavy earth wall, but it is a practical way to take in views and to air the building out.

The sheen of steel and glass components reflects the landscape, and all together these aspects make the building ephemeral and nearly invisible at certain times of day.

"It is hard to take a picture of it because it blends into

ABOVE: The rammed-earth building literally reflects the landscape. RIGHT: The earth for the wall came from the site. The Felt chair is by Marc Newson. FACING: The master suite is on the left; guest cottages are on the right.

a building that was thrilling and yet in tune with the land.

"We walked around for days. We stared in one direction and then in the other. We did it in June and then in October and then in March before spring," Nave said. "We watched herds of elk and picked up pieces of sage and tried to make that into architecture."

Nave and his team made sketches and many models with the site as their muse. As they studied the terrain, they discovered that its arid soil was rich in aggregate suited for rammed earth and decided to use it in a special mix of portland cement and soil.

Such a house that invokes the spirit of its site, and quite literally springs from it, is rare. The 60-foot rammed-earth

the land. If you were to stand out there you could miss it. Most of the time it looks like rock outcroppings and shadows that exist in the landscape," Nave said, pleased with its success. "It is a lesson in how to build in a vast landscape and not make a lightbulb that calls attention to itself." □

BELOW AND RIGHT: Japanese-style sliding doors from the master bedroom to a lower-level den and office save space. The double-sided fireplace, seen in both rooms, is clad in steel. A deck, seen through glass doors, extends the space.

Ski country in British Columbia, Canada.

Resort Cabin, British Columbia

BOHLIN CYWINSKI JACKSON

"We really wanted to be right on those mountain slopes so we could spend a lot of time there," a telecommunications lawyer from Calgary, Alberta, said. He and his wife, a former café owner, had been smitten after skiing at a remote resort in the western Rocky Mountains—an easy two-and-a-half-hour drive west from their home—and they envisioned tranquil weekends there with their three children.

The spot the couple found so irresistible is near the confluence of the Columbia and Kicking Horse rivers, where majestic peaks overlook scenic Banff, Glacier, Jasper, Kootenay and Yoho national parks. They purchased a narrow, gently sloping lot amid spruce and aspen forests near the base of a ski trail that disappears into mists 8,000 feet above sea level, and began to think of a special retreat.

LEFT: The roof and operable wall panels are of painted steel.
ABOVE: Single-story living spaces are connected by a bridge to a two-story bedroom wing.
OVERLEAF: The kitchen, on the main floor of the bedroom wing, is aligned with the living and dining spaces.

"I had worked at back country lodges and knew what would function best, but we knew better than to design the house ourselves," the wife said.

They chose the Seattle design office of Bohlin Cywinski Jackson, whose modernist work they had previously admired, and described their vision. It didn't include a typical wood-framed log house.

Principal designer Ray Calabro recalls their first meeting. "The husband brought along a folder full of images they had collected and methodically gave us the size of large living spaces. But his wife said it should feel small, like a 1970s James Bond ski chalet in Scandinavia," Calabro said. "So we simply married their ideas for an edgy cabin in the forest."

His design colleagues, Kyle Phillips and Robert Miller, and firm principal Peter Bohlin, who also worked on the 3,700-square-foot design, concurred that in the spacious vistas and gargantuan mountains of the still wild West, as Calabro said, "people are open-minded and will consider designs that people from other places won't."

They created two wings to fit between the biggest trees and added a covered bridge and stairwell between them. Front stairs to the bridge are on axis with a rear landing on the higher west slope for easy access to ski trails.

The south structure is small, elevated and trapezoidal, with an open-plan living and dining space. The other wing, along the north edge of the property, is a densely programmed, shed-roofed, bar-shaped form, cantilevered over poured-concrete foundation walls. It contains a central kitchen in line with the living spaces, and bedrooms and baths on either end that can be closed off by pocket doors. In its attic, three built-in bunk beds have large adult-size mattresses for the children and their friends, because "we know that in the blink of an eye our kids will be fully grown," the wife said.

"We wanted to articulate each wing in two different ways," Calabro said. The smaller one is like a traditional

RIGHT: Dark floors contrast with Douglas fir plywood-clad walls and beech furniture by Naoto Fukasawa.

LEFT: Custom ladder stairs lead to loft bedrooms in the attic.
BOTTOM: A handy inset bench by the back door.
FACING: Roomy bunks for children have queen mattresses.

single-story cabin with a metal shed roof and stained cedar siding. Its unusual form floats above the dense snow pack in the winter, and it seems anchored to its site by a tall concrete fireplace on the south wall. The cabin's lively Douglas fir plywood-clad walls and ceiling extend beyond picture windows in back, framing alpine views and sheltering an outdoor deck.

As counterpoint, the taller pavilion has a crisp standing seam painted steel shed roof, which folds down over its south wall. Operable flaps in the wall allow air into the attic.

The limited material palette meets the resort's stringent rules, which were tweaked only slightly by the architects.

"We pushed the boundaries," Calabro said. For instance, when resort managers called for textured concrete to simulate stone, the architects suggested board-formed concrete. Since muted natural colors were allowed, the architects chose a native wildflower red to accent the building. Metal for exterior cladding is prohibited, therefore their metal wall leans in slightly up top so that it can be considered a part of the roof.

Other design details are also practical yet lyrical. Pocket doors match the wall siding indoors so they "disappear" even when they are in use. Hardy stained cedar and Cor-Ten steel wall cladding mimic the tertiary colors of the woods, and deep window seats in all the bedrooms double as twin beds when guests arrive with little children.

Other rooms are also intended to be multifunctional. The master bedroom has three window seat beds, and a playroom with a Murphy bed in the basement of the longer structure can be transformed into an extra guest room.

"We wanted a small mountain cabin that could be flexible and fun for our family and friends instead of a large house with regular amenities," the wife said. "When you cram sixteen people in a tiny space it also forces a kind of intimacy and deeper engagement for years to come." □

Truckee House, California

JOHN MANISCALCO ARCHITECTURE

"The first time we saw Sugar Bowl, the place had magic for us," Maca Huneeus said.

An avid skier, she grew up near Andean slopes in Chile, and she and her vintner husband, Agustin, now consider this Depression-era ski resort in the Sierras the place to be each winter when Quintessa, the award-winning Huneeus family winery in the Napa Valley, lies dormant.

The couple visited the slopes as guests for several years until they chanced upon a rare unbuilt lot in the old village, a bastion of Alpine homes for several generations of Californians. The house they tucked into their choice site "is

LEFT: Living spaces on top have grandstand views. Snow levels typically rise to the entrance. BELOW: The roof, designed to shed snow in back, also protects slit windows.

ski-in, ski-out, a real privilege," Huneeus said.

That advantage—made possible by the extraordinary amounts of snow that fall on those slopes—posed particular challenges for San Francisco architect John Maniscalco, who was hired to design a modern house that could function year-round for the Huneeuses and their four young girls.

Designing such a house for extreme weather conditions was hard enough without the added complication of making it a contemporary house that could fit in amid steeply gabled Swiss chalet–style structures that abound there.

Luckily, Maniscalco had worked previously on modernizing the Huneeus's San Francisco Edwardian, and he knew how to marry old and new in ways that they would enjoy.

"Modern for me is simple grandeur," Huneeus said. Growing up in Zapallar, along Chile's Valparaiso coast, her parents had a concrete house with practical built-in seating, a collection of furniture by Alvar Aalto and Le Corbusier, and expressionistic, surrealist paintings by Roberto Matta. They instilled in her a love of spare, functional forms and controlled spatial theatrics.

Maniscalco funneled those ideas into a pragmatic 3,800-square-foot design. He calculated the average depth of snowpacks each year, and designed two eight-foot-high concrete plinths that elevate the house—made up of two stacked south-facing boxes—just above the snow.

"Agustin and Maca disembark from the gondola that brings them across the valley and ride a Sno-Cat right up to their front door," Maniscalco beams.

Aesthetically, the house fits neatly between old and new. The lower cedar-clad box resembles conventional hunkered-down mountain cabins, while above it sits a modern glassy

FACING: A showy fireplace anchors the living spaces. French doors (not visible) open to a loggia on the left.
RIGHT, TOP: In the kitchen, slit windows have views of the wooded mountains. Counters and an island base are of Corian.
RIGHT: The wood-clad central stairwell.

FACING: Maniscalco designed twin bunk beds for the children's room on the lower floor. RIGHT: In the master suite, cedar-clad walls echo the woods visible through French doors facing the front. BOTTOM: A deep soaking tub.

box with asymmetrical bays and wonderful valley views.

The building's sloped zinc shed roof is designed to fold down sharply to clad the back wall. It looks dramatic, but it is also smart. Engineered to support heavy loads of snow and ice, the gently back-sloping roof—like many railroad sheds in the avalanche-prone area—sheds melted snow in back, away from passersby. The sludge has room to flow through between the plinths. At the main entrance, wide roof overhangs offer added protection from falling snow.

The first floor is in many respects a utilitarian, inward-looking bunker. Its recessed porch leads to a vestibule and a double-story stairwell between a mudroom and service rooms on the right, and rooms for guests and a loft-like children's room fitted with bunk beds on the left.

Upstairs, however, the master suite and living spaces with glass doors that open to loggias command memorable snowy vistas seven months of the year. When the sun shines into these unshuttered rooms, which are purposely set back a few feet from the front for privacy, they are ablaze with light.

Slit windows in the zinc-clad north kitchen wall provide glancing views of the woods, the snow and the mountains.

Maniscalco's finishes bring the landscape inside as well. Ceilings, walls and custom cabinets are of Douglas fir. Walnut planking for floors and end-grain butcher-block counters are additional arboreal details, all accented by an island base and kitchen countertops of snowy white Caesarstone.

"I wanted the mountain to be felt at all times," Huneeus emphasized.

Not surprisingly, she handpicked earth-toned wool and leather furnishings because they are tough enough to handle kids with ski gear on, but also because they evoke nature's magic outdoors. □

Artist Ann Hamilton's Tower at the Oliver Ranch near Geyserville, California.

contains a giant madrone tree growing high above a sloping meadow. The enclave incorporates a 3,000-square-foot rectangular main house connected by a Cor-Ten-covered, concrete-walled loggia spine to a couple of matching but smaller guest pavilions and a swimming pool. Another path also links the main house to a 1,200-square-foot recreation room equipped with bunk beds for the couple's grandchildren.

"We often invite friends but also love going up there just the two of us," the wife said. "When we are by ourselves we only open the main house and are not forced to walk down empty hallways past closed bedroom doors."

The shed roofs of the guest pavilions, anchored on the low side to the loggia's concrete entablature, hinge up to maximize views. The roofs are held high by slender steel braces at the upper end, and clear glass walls fill the space between the roof and floor planes for vistas from inside. From outside, "the glass also literally reflects the landscape," Schuh said. That's why, at certain times of day, the buildings, cantilevered over high retaining walls of stone and concrete, seem to disappear into a backdrop of undisturbed woods on the south side and naturalistic swaths of drought-tolerant grasses planted nearby. On the north side, pastures cascade into a valley and creep up the opposite slope.

"My husband wanted to take advantage of the view. He wanted to walk into the house and see hills and meadows instantly and that is exactly what happens," the wife said.

"In the morning we watch the fog settle down like a blanket and then lift up with the sun."

Quite satisfyingly, as shrouded trees are unveiled slowly and the primitive landscape "comes into focus," she added, "there is no hint of busy vineyards just minutes away." □

FACING: A bedroom with views of the woods has a modern Arne Jacobsen floor lamp and Saarinen Womb chair.
RIGHT, TOP AND BOTTOM: The children's pavilion has stairs shaded by a slatted wood screen.

Calistoga Art Cave, California

BADE STAGEBERG COX

Art collectors Norah and Norman Stone weren't looking to add rooms to their 2,000-square-foot Victorian farmhouse in Calistoga, an hour north of the Golden Gate Bridge, even though it had become another repository for their burgeoning collection, which started 25 years ago in their San Francisco mansion that is now brimming with blue-chip Warhols and includes works by Jeff Koons, Bruce Nauman, Sigmar Polke and Joseph Beuys.

"We continue to collect more art from our times," Norman Stone, a scion of late insurance magnate William Clement Stone and a San Francisco Museum of Modern Art trustee, said. Among the artists the Stones support under the direction of New York art consultant Thea Westreich are Matias Faldbakken, Ryan Gander and Taryn Simon, who are all in their 30s.

FACING: The entry to the art cave cuts into the hillside. ABOVE: Cady Noland's *Log Cabin Blank with Screw Eyes and Café Door*. TOP RIGHT: The Stones' Victorian farmhouse. RIGHT: In the exit gallery, videos by Bruce Conner. OVERLEAF: In the entry gallery, works by Rirkrit Tiravanija and Vito Acconci.

"But we did not want another big house for art," Norah Stone, also an SFMOMA trustee, said. "We like the cozy, intimate scale of the cottage, whose elements came straight out of an 1878 Sears Roebuck catalog. I have spent happy summers on our farm in western Canada, where I am from, and it reminds me of that."

Nonetheless, seeking more room to display their collection, the adventurous, trendsetting pair commissioned a 5,700-square-foot cave near the house. The first of its kind, the art cave is burrowed into a hillside that borders their 17-acre vineyard. It adds to the Stones's growing stash of conceptual art in the country, which includes an outdoor sculpture by Cady Noland called *Log Cabin Blank with Screw Eyes and Café Door,* an angled sculpture of Cor-Ten steel by Richard Serra called *Square Level Forged,* and *Stone Sky, 2005,* an experiential LED light sculpture by James Turrell that hovers above and within a swimming pool.

The ingenious art cave with its own complicated palette

ABOVE: Richard Serra's *Square Level Forged* and *Black Triangle.*
RIGHT: Ceiling lights by Mike Renfro Designs. Mike Kelly's *Shift* (on the floor) and *Antiqued,* a vintage bureau, adjoin *Feet Don't Fail Me Now,* a work on paper by Christopher Wool. Dan Flavin's *The Diagonal of May 25,* a fluorescent tube, is on the wall.

of lights mounted to the ceiling was designed by New York architects Bade Stageberg Cox. A tunnel roadheader, typically used for excavating caves for wine storage, formed the "U" shape of the brightly lit, white-painted, vaulted interior. Weathering steel and glass doors seal in the art when there is no audience of invited fellow collectors and museum groups lucky enough to be shown the rotating works—some of which are too big to display in most galleries and museums.

Significant interruptions to cabernet sauvignon wine production were inevitable during the construction of the art cave, the pool installation, and the planting of swaths of lavender and other landscaping gestures by Tom Leader Studio. However, the Stones used the lull in viticultural activity on their estate to refurbish the interior of the old farmhouse.

Former owners, who introduced odd marble bathrooms and new flooring, had removed original fixtures from the historic cottage, whose structural timbers were no doubt cut from a stand of redwoods right on the property.

The Stones undid the poor additions in stages, starting with the return of old heart pine floors, and eventually filled the refurbished space with midcentury Scandinavian furniture and pieces by Finn Juhl, Ib Kofod-Larsen and Alvar Aalto, all curated by Westreich. San Francisco interior designer Charles de Lisle redid the country kitchen, installed a new fireplace and devised a glass picture window that is both a "canvas" for decals by Lawrence Weiner and a spot to view Turrell's custom skyspace at night from inside the house.

"The changes were important," Norman said. "With the art in the cave, the house feels larger and the simple modern environment is a better expression of our artistic interest now. We use the furniture we collect in the house. It is all pure and simple and particularly relaxing." ◻

FACING: Above the bed designed by Alfredo Häberli is artist Robert Beck's *Screen Memory (Mother's Room)*.
TOP RIGHT: The attic bedroom has views of the valley.
RIGHT: Cheyney Thompson art and a Hans Wegner chair.

Paso Robles Ranch, California

AIDLIN DARLING DESIGN

When San Francisco architect Joshua Aidlin first saw the acres of rolling hills and prairie near Paso Robles in Southern California that belong to a law professor and her husband, he went camping.

"I went with Peter Larsen from my office and we spent the night just below the highest ridge in our sleeping bags and tents with coyotes howling around us," Aidlin recalls.

The first purple light revealed a dramatic valley shielded by low rolling hills from the main road and from neighboring farms and vineyards. In thrall to the setting, the two architects pushed down stakes to mark the spot for their clients, who live in Washington, D.C., most of the year.

The owners wanted an asymmetrical retreat like the ranch house in East Hampton, New York, where the husband, an environmental lawyer, had spent many a summer.

The compact, 2,660-square-foot, H-shaped house Aidlin and his team at Aidlin Darling Design created comprises two long unequal but parallel wings connected by a small rectangular foyer. It is primarily a direct response to Aidlin and Larsen's shared experience on the site.

Set on a slightly canted east-west axis, it gets sunlight all day. The first light fills the master bedroom, the afternoon sun bathes a dining loggia facing the valley and in the evening the sun creeps into living spaces on the west end. The staggered but parallel public and private wings, defined by cinder-block walls, are separated by a slender interior courtyard and nestled so low to the ground "that all you see are roof planes floating above the horizon," Aidlin said.

"The cinder-block walls are like 'ruins' in the ground and we have essentially inserted living spaces within them," Aidlin said. The flat roofs, pierced by a concrete-block chimney that anchors the building to the ridgeline, hover over wood-frame walls inside and exterior walls and posts of tough Cor-Ten steel that can weather harsh, cold winters.

Since the owners and their young son only use the house during breaks when they are not back East, "we needed a

LEFT: Concrete-block walls for the house are like "ruins" in the landscape according to Aidlin. The carport roof stretches back over bedrooms between the ruins.

FACING: A central concrete-block wall separates the bedroom wing on the left from the public areas and guest room facing the valley on the right. A low vestibule with a door of Cor-Ten steel sits between the long, parallel wings.

OVERLEAF: A view of the public wing facing the valley. A loggia and outdoor fireplace are on the right next to a low-walled swimming court designed to keep wildlife out.

LEFT: An outdoor chimney and a sliding metal fence separate a spa and swimming pool courtyard from the kitchen loggia. The pool is protected from wildlife by a low wall on the left and a Cor-Ten fence abutting the master bedroom on the right.
BOTTOM: A dining loggia with a fireplace off the kitchen has valley views. Steps on the left go up to the metal pool gate.

maintenance-free skin that required no painting and had no boards warping on the exterior," Aidlin said.

Roof-mounted photovoltaic panels harness the sun's heat and in-floor hydronic systems circulate it. Water from wells is used for minimal, naturalistic landscaping and for filling the swimming pool at the east end of the sustainable building. Concrete decks around the living area and pool, interspersed with native plantings and stepping stones, help to integrate the house into its setting.

In materials and form, the staggered, single-story, concrete-block structure clearly echoes Mies van der Rohe's

buildings, as well as Frank Lloyd Wright's prefab Usonian houses that Rudolph M. Schindler and Richard Neutra later emulated in Los Angeles. It is also not unlike many tin-roofed adobe farm buildings nearby.

Inside, a palette of natural materials including chocolate brown ipe wood on the floors, vertical grain rift oak for

ABOVE: A Fritz Hansen PK20 easy chair designed by Poul Kjaerholm; a doorway leads to the guest bedroom.
RIGHT: Inside the vestibule, a partially visible oak wood-clad closet is for storing wine. A green B&B Italia couch designed by Antonio Citterio complements *Rose Window,* a Glen Baldridge diptych from Guerrero Gallery. Eileen Gray-esque chairs sit around a table by Citterio.

cabinets, and cream-colored cinder-block walls and white paint is also maintenance free. Brightly colored furniture accents this tertiary scheme.

In the small rectangular vestibule that links the two wings, a freestanding, oak-clad, climate-controlled wine room in the shape of a cube defines the center of the house, and also serves to remind the owners of their dream to plant their own vineyard when they move in permanently.

"It was going to be just a holiday home, but at the end of every summer they simply hate to leave," Aidlin said. ☐

ABOVE: The glass-walled eastside master bedroom has new furniture by OHIO Design and art by John Trenholm Abrahams. The outdoor cinder-block shower stall gets the first light.
RIGHT: The master bathroom has a double sink and a shower with a second door that connects it to the outdoor shower.

Geyserville Studios, California

JIM JENNINGS ARCHITECTURE

As art patrons Nancy and Steve Oliver's ambition for a sculpture park on their 100-acre Sonoma County sheep ranch near Geyserville grew, so did the scale of the projects they commissioned, which included large site-specific steel works by Richard Serra and irregular hillside stairs of concrete by Bruce Nauman. For visiting artists who needed a place to stay on the ranch while they contemplated how best to engage with the land, the Olivers envisioned two guest studios atop a hill close to their weekend residence designed by architect Robert Overstreet, a protégé of Bruce Goff.

LEFT: One of the skylit studios. ABOVE: Two imperceptibly converging retaining walls double as side walls for nearly identical twin studios ensconced between them.

However, when they asked their friend Jim Jennings, an award-winning minimalist San Francisco architect to design the studios, he suggested sinking the buildings into the hill where they could have views to the north as well as the south.

"One of Jim's favorite installations on the ranch that was completed in 1989 is *Russian River Bones* (a skeletal wood construction) by Robert Stackhouse," Steve Oliver said.

It became Jennings's "true north," even though it lies south of the site. He picked a 20-foot-wide spot on the north side of the hill where the Olivers wanted to build and drew a long, narrow triangle—like a fixed compass needle—that converges on Stackhouse's sculpture in the distance.

BELOW: A third retaining wall is for stairs that descend to an opening in the east wall and a central courtyard.
RIGHT: The walled courtyard is between the two studios.

"Then Jim asked us to cut away a 150-foot-long, 12-foot-deep wedge-shaped chunk of the hill that was within the slender triangle," Oliver said.

Jennings's intention was not so much to make site-specific art as to have a functioning building in the site without creating any "visual conflict" with what was already there. He wanted the studios to be invisible.

At the time, it was a formidable task even for Steve Oliver's eponymous construction company. Soon after the design won a 1992 Progressive Architecture Award he pushed the pause button for several years—distracted in part by his positions on the board of trustees of the San Francisco Museum of Modern Art, the California College of the Arts and other arts organizations. In the interim he got the idea of pairing Jennings with New York sculptor David Rabinowitch, a friend of the late artist Donald Judd, to create habitable art objects instead of mere buildings.

"I thought the concrete retaining walls we'd have to build to hold back the hill on each side of the slot could be a canvas for David's carved work. It would showcase Jim's work as well as what my company could accomplish," Oliver said. In 1998, the shelved design enhanced with Rabinowitch's work came back to life and received more acclaim when it was completed in 2003, proving its timelessness.

"There was no change. In the early 1990s it was a schematic design. In 2001 we had structural engineers, and walls were thickened slightly because David's 2½-inch-deep carving came into play," Jennings said.

The two trapezoidal artist studios of carved concrete and clear glass walls are set at each end of their long, narrow artificial ravine in the hill, and are separated by a small gravel-filled courtyard they share in the middle. Because the studios sit on the widest part of Jennings's extremely long triangular plan, the east and west walls converge so imperceptibly that they seem to be parallel at first glance. To compensate for the slightly reduced floor space in the narrower south studio, Jennings made its floor lower by a few inches

FACING: Lowered floors in the narrower studio allow the volumes and ceiling heights of both studios to be the same.
TOP AND ABOVE: Jenning's subtly different room dimensions and Rabinowitch's free-form wall incisions are balanced by designer Gary Hutton's matching interiors.

so that the volume of each studio is exactly the same. The ceilings in both studios are at precisely the same elevation, adding to the illusion of sameness.

"The building is made by first cutting out a space for them. That cut in the hill is open at both ends and also open

TOP: A tiny kitchenette and bathroom are behind the headboard. ABOVE: Steel bridges between the walls carry the weight of the roof and allow for unbroken slits in the roof for skylights on each side. They also conceal LED lights.
FACING: Each bedroom has its own private exit.

above," Jennings explains. The concrete walls that imperceptibly converge southward hold the hill back, and steel bridges that go from east to west form roofs for the two studios. Their steel armature and posts make it possible to have ribbon skylights uninterrupted by framing between the floating ceilings and the sidewalls. Natural light floods in all day long on each side, animating Rabinowitch's swirling, arabesque lines carved into the concrete surface and throwing some parts into shadow and others into high focus. At night a strip of fiber-optic lights inset at the bottom of the concrete walls inside and out creates a different effect—one that allows stars or the moon above to have greater visibility.

A kitchen, bath and fireplace are freestanding pieces in the center of each building so that Rabinowitch's "cosmic" graffiti is uninterrupted as it flows freely from the north studio through the courtyard and into the south studio.

Peculiarly, the ideas these modern buildings embody are at least as old as ancient Rome's Vitruvius, who described in his *Ten Books of Architecture* the interaction between the "light of heavenly bodies" and architecture, and the effects that distance, foreshortening and sculptural relief on flat surfaces have on buildings.

When you climb up the hill from the main house, the west wall, which rises higher than the hill, obscures the buildings from view. A set of opposing staircases lead down through a narrow opening in the wall into the central courtyard, "but it is also possible to enter each of the studios from the outer ends of the long cut in the hill," Jennings said.

Conversely, it is possible to look through the north and south glass walls of both buildings at the view on each side. In this way Jennings has subtly linked Stackhouse's metaphorical sculpture to a lake just north of the site that is like a fragment of the Russian River meandering nearby.

Even if there were no intent to make these twin Euclidian sky-lit shelters, one slightly wider than the other, into site-specific art, they are at least light-capturing vessels, instruments to measure distance and to look at the natural terrain.

"Yes, the complete building is a perceptual telescope," Jennings said. "And I am glad that, because of David's work, the entire building is considered part of his sculpture. The architectural concept will always remain whole. In this case art is put in the service of architecture." □

St. Helena Retreat, California

ERIN MARTIN DESIGN

The historic water tower on Andy and Sharon Gillin's property outside St. Helena, California, was probably just being finished when writer Robert Louis Stevenson came to the restorative hot springs in Napa Valley with his new bride in 1880 and wrote his travel memoir *The Silverado Squatters*.

Stevenson describes a derelict mining camp on the shoulder of Mount Saint Helena in the Mayacamas Mountains that became their home for two months. They added makeshift linen window coverings and supplied it with buckets of stream water and wine from Schramsberg Vineyards.

It was this kind of hippie, West Coast splendor that the Gillins, who live in Piedmont, California, aspired to for the two wings they added on either side of their three-story tower with the help of architect Wayne Leong.

Wings on two sides of the tower form an L-shape that contains a courtyard. They are composed of a series of simple stucco-clad boxes with alternating flat and gabled roofs that mimic the silhouette of vernacular farmhouses in the valley and create the illusion of a compound that grew by accretion.

A vestibule in the longer north-facing wing is almost on axis with a swimming pool in the courtyard, and a great room with exposed rafters, a kitchen with clerestory windows, and an enfilade of an office and three small bedrooms all have steel French doors that open to the central space.

To infuse the simplified shapes with local flavor, Sharon Gillin, a retired psychologist with a bent for interior design, had begun to shop at designer Erin Martin's home furnishings store on Main Street in St. Helena even before the

FACING: New wings that form a sheltering "L" around a swimming pool flank the refurbished three-story water tower.
TOP AND RIGHT: The front door opens to a roomy vestibule that also leads to the courtyard and living room with a fireplace.

FACING: In the guest bedroom, Martin's design credo is at work: white walls, black steel details, quiet textiles and patches of bold color. RIGHT: An Agape bathtub and inset towel storage. BOTTOM: The tower's red spiral stair.

weekend house was ready. Before long, Gillin even brought the designer home to help her complete the design.

Quirky objects of stone, unfinished wood, glass, forged metal and cloth like those Stevenson describes in his book—all ingredients of Martin's typical gutsy palette for clients in Napa as well as the technology Valhalla of Silicon Valley—soon brought visual cohesion and character to the rooms.

"My palette is for bare feet, grandchildren and living life in general," Martin said. "That has staying power."

To unify Gillin's disparate collection of objects, Martin introduced some recurring handcrafted elements. "The house was boxy, and needed to be softened. I wanted something layered with textures and a continuous jazzy rhythm. A little like John Coltrane's music," Martin explained.

White plaster walls by San Francisco artisan Terry Bryant juxtaposed with oiled walnut doors from Evan Shively in Petaluma, furnishings, including a fireplace surround and wood storage bin of steel forged by JJ Forge in Middletown and a metal table base made by Mick Handley from Santa Barbara are all a nod to California's timeless Mission style.

"I also love natural forms that can be used as art. I am equally infatuated by artists like Anish Kapoor," Martin said, as if to explain her choices that range from weathered, sun-bleached found objects to sculpted blocks of pure color.

For instance, she added an exciting red metal spiral staircase to connect the various levels of the restored water tower.

Martin also responded to Gillin's taste for rich textiles with a variety of fabrics, some of them custom, in every room.

"Interior design is part gut feeling and art, but it can also be mathematical," Martin said, divulging a secret. "If you just use wood, stone, metal and glass consistently and something dark to ground it all, that's all you really need." □

Resources

ARCHITECTS, DESIGNERS, FURNITURE: A WEB DIRECTORY

Aidlin Darling Design: aidlin-darling-design.com
Allied Works Architecture: alliedworks.com
Andrea Cochran Landscape Architecture: acochran.com
Arkitektura: arksf.com
B&B Italia: bb-sf.com
Bade Stageberg Cox: bscarchitecture.com
BattersbyHowat Architects: battersbyhowat.com
Bellomo Architects: bellomoarchitects.com
blank studio architecture: blankspaces.net
Blue Sky Architecture: blueskyarchitecture.com
Bohlin Cywinski Jackson: bcj.com
Cary Bernstein Architect: cbstudio.com
CCS Architecture: CCS-architecture.com
Charles de Lisle Workshop: cdlworkshop.com
Concreteworks: concreteworks.com
Craig Steely Architecture: craigsteely.com
Daly Genik Architects: dalygenik.com
De Sousa Hughes: desousahughes.com
Design Within Reach: dwr.com
Dowling Studios: dowling-studios.com
DZINE: dzinestore.com
Eames Foundation: eamesfoundation.org
Edward Fields Carpet Makers: edwardfields.com
EHDD: ehdd.com
Ehrlich Architects: ehrlicharchitects.com
Eggleston|Farkas Architects: eggfarkarch.com
Erin Martin Design: erinmartindesign.com
Eye on Design by Dan Gregory: blog.houseplans.com
Feldman Architecture: feldmanarchitecture.com
Fernau & Hartman Architects: fernauhartman.com
Flos: flosusa.com
Fougeron Architecture: fougeron.com
Fritz Hansen: fritzhansen.com
Gary Hutton Design: garyhuttondesign.com
Gemmill Design: gemmilldesign.com
Gubi: gubi.dk
Herman Miller: hermanmiller.com
Interstice Architects: intersticearchitects.com
Jensen Architects: jensen-architects.com
Jim Jennings Architecture: jimjenningsarchitecture.com
JJ Forge: jjforge.com
John Maniscalco Architecture: m-architecture.com
Jonathan Browning Studios: jonathanbrowninginc.com
Karim Rashid: karimrashid.com
Knoll: knoll.com
Konstantin Grcic: konstantin-grcic.com
Kuth/Ranieri Architects: kuthranieri.com
Lake|Flato Architects: lakeflato.com
Legorreta + Legorreta: legorretalegorreta.com

Leong Architects: leongarch.com
Leddy Maytum Stacy Architects: lmsarch.com
Lorcan O'Herlihy Architects (LOHA): loharchitects.com
Lorissa Kimm Architect: lorissakimm.com
Macy Architecture: macyarchitecture.com
Marmol Radziner: marmol-radziner.com
Matthew Millman: matthewmillman.com
Mayer Sattler-Smith: mayersattler-smith.com
Melander Architects, Inc.: melanderarchitects.com
Michael P. Johnson Design Studio: mpjstudio.com
Minotti: minotti.com
Moroso: moroso.it
Nana Wall Systems: nanawall.com
Naoto Fukasawa Design: naotofukasawa.com
Nick Noyes Architecture: nnarchitecture.com
NICOLEHOLLIS: nicolehollis.com
Nielsen:Schuh Architects: nielsenschuh.com
Ogrydziak/Prillinger Architects: oparch.net
OHIO Design: ohiodesign.com
Oliver Ranch Foundation: oliverranchfoundation.org
Olson Kundig Architects: olsonkundigarchitects.com
Pfau Long Architecture: pfaulong.com
Philpotts Interiors: philpotts.net
Phoenix Day: phoenixday.com
RAIS: rais.com
RHEINZINK: rheinzink.com
Renfro Design Group: renfrodesign.com
Rick Joy Architects: www.rickjoy.com
The Rug Company: therugcompany.info/index.htm
Sally Ward Interiors: sallywardinteriors.com
Stanley Saitowitz | Natoma Architects, Inc.: saitowitz.com
Steven Miller Design Studio: stevenmillerdesignstudio.com
Stremmel Gallery: stremmelgallery.com
Stryker Sonoma Winery: strykersonoma.com
Studio.bna: studio-bna.com
Swatt | Miers Architects: swattmiers.com
Terry & Terry Architecture: terryandterryarchitecture.com
Terry Hunziker Inc.: terryhunziker.com
Thea Westreich Art Advisory Services: twaas.com
Therien & Co. Studio Workshops: therien.com/SW_SITE/index.php
Tom Leader Studio: tomleader.com
Turnbull Griffin Haeesloop: tgharchitects.com
Vitra: vitra.com
Walker Warner Architects: walker-warner.com
The Wiseman Group: wisemangroup.com
Zack | de Vito: zackdevito.com
Zahid Sardar: @designspot (Twitter)
Zinc Details: zincdetails.com
Zographos Designs Limited: zographos.com

Acknowledgments

CONTRIBUTORS AND BIBLIOGRAPHY

A NOTE FROM THE AUTHOR:

My grateful thanks to all the homeowners, architects and designers who so generously allowed us into their houses and told us their inspiring stories.

Thanks also to Gibbs Smith, Suzanne Taylor and Madge Baird for their confidence in this book and to our eagle-eyed editor Bob Cooper, who has been patient and persevering.

Plaudits to interior designer Agnes Bourne in Jackson Hole and Erin Cullerton, founder of Design Agency Co. in Los Angeles, for steering us to projects we might have missed.

Lastly, a round of applause goes to Michael Wollaeger of *Interiors Magazine.* As founding editor of *Western Interiors & Design,* the first magazine to properly define the modern West, he introduced us to his vision and provided a unique forum to celebrate West Coast design.

BELOW: A bent bamboo *objet* for a Hawaii house by architects Legorreta + Legorreta and designer Paul Wiseman.
OVERLEAF: For Chara Schreyer's home in Tiburon, California, designer Gary Hutton added Foscarini's Tosca table lamp alongside Scott Hug's framed JFK photograph on the wall.

A NOTE FROM THE PHOTOGRAPHER:

First and foremost, I want to thank my wife, Megan Werner, for all of her support.

Additionally, I would like to thank Kurt Lundquist, James Newman, Tom Tomkinson, G. Todd Roberts and LeAnn Raschke for their assistance with the photography in this book, and Dina Dobkin for her help researching projects. I would also like to thank Grant Mudford, Richard Barnes, Tim Street-Porter and Christopher Irion for their guidance over the years.

Finally, I want to thank and acknowledge editor Michael Wollaeger and his work. It was through the great projects he asked me to photograph for *Western Interiors & Design* that this book was born.

SELECTED BIBLIOGRAPHY:

Gregory, Daniel, *Cliff May and the Modern Ranch House.* Rizzoli, 2008.

Lyndon, Donlyn, and Jim Alinder, *The Sea Ranch.* Princeton Architectural Press, 2004.

Steele, James, *Los Angeles Architecture: The Contemporary Condition.* Phaidon, 1993.

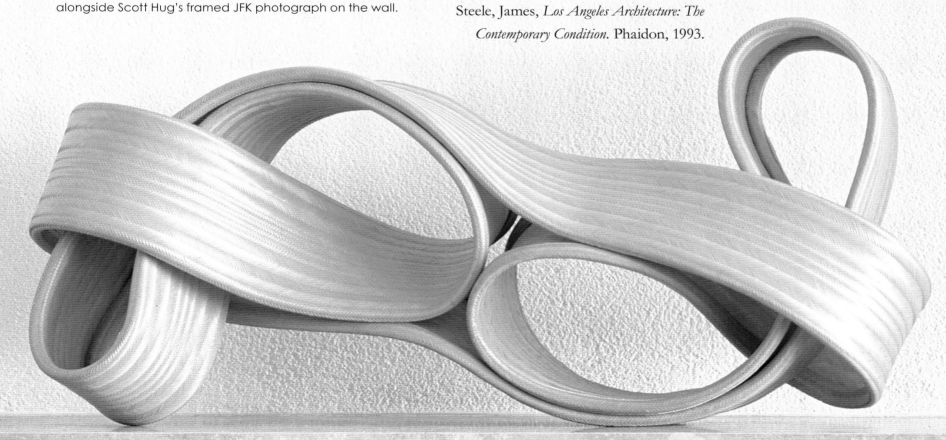